SECOND MARRIAGE

BY
Jonell H. Kirby, Ed.D.
Counseling and Guidance Department
West Virginia College of Graduate Studies
Institute, West Virginia

62157

Accelerated Development Inc.
P.O. Box 667
Muncie, Indiana 47305
Tel. (317) 284-7511

Library of Congress Catalog Card Number: 78-74004

International Standard Book Number: 0-915202-18-2

Corporate Editor: Linda K. Davis

Graphic Artist: Mary J. Blizzard

Printed in the United States of America, June 1979

For additional copies order from

Accelerated Development Inc.
2515 W. Jackson Street
Muncie, In 47305
Tel. (317) 284-7511

Dedicated to Joe
my compeer, friend
and helper.

FOREWORD

Much attention is given to marriage, but little of this attention has been directed toward second marriages. I believe that the dynamics of relationships are the same in both instances; however, the influence of external forces is greater on second marriages, and the problems and potential problems confronting the couple are more apparent in the second marriage. The second marriage represents a crisis in the social process.

Second marriage offers a good opportunity to study one's own behavior and its impact on others. It is a reasonable time to assess one's potential influence on the several social systems, such as the family, which will result from the marriage.

Second Marriage is partly my story and partly the story of all those people involved with me: my family, friends, and clients. My husband has spent long hours discussing with me the concepts and suggestions I have included in this book. My children have been a source of information and have offered encouraging support in my efforts. All of these people have been my teachers and they have made my life fuller and richer. They have made me want to share some of myself and my thoughts about second marriage. To some extent, *Second Marriage* is about all of us, our living together, our loving one another, and our interpersonal relationships.

Almost everyone is involved in second marriage at some level. If you are into or anticipating such a marriage, then I hope you will garner strength and courage by knowing you are not alone. If you have friends involved, then one goal for the book is to help you gain some insight and sensitivity so as to make your friendship more supportive. If you are a family related member of individuals undergoing the agony and ecstasy of this new and meaningful relationship, then a second goal I have is that by your reading this book you will gain an appreciation of the intensity of the emotions and the knowledge for closer ties and stronger relationships. A third goal is that the thoughts contained herein will make us all more aware of our own values, needs, and interrelatedness and that through this understanding, we will be more warmly human and accepting of ourselves and others.

This book would not be complete without some words of appreciation and comments concerning people who have made major contributions to me and my thinking. My special appreciation is expressed to my husband, Joe, who has supported me in so many ways; to my children, Sylvia, Gloria and David; and to my son-in-law Sherif, all of whom have contributed immeasurably to my happiness and to *Second Marriage*. I owe a debt to my friends and the friends of my children who have continued to enrich my life and keep me involved in their lives. These persons are too numerous to name individually, but it does not make the expression less sincere. Although they too are included in this last mentioned group, I am especially grateful to Ina Ruth Scott and Colette Dolen for their assistance in typing and retyping the manuscript; to Jan Penix-Mayhew for her editorial and technical assistance; to Doris Colomb, Bill and Betty Pittman, Julia Kelly, and Dr. Bill Hayes, Psychiatrist, who reacted to the manuscript and influenced its final form. My present and former students as well as my former teachers are reflected in my thoughts as surely as my parents, brothers and sisters, because these people have influenced who I am and what I think. Therefore, my manuscript is partly their manuscript and my contribution becomes in part theirs. I appreciate these influences and their personal support.

TABLE OF CONTENTS

LIST OF FIGURES

CHAPTER 1

THE SECOND MARRIAGE
PARADOXES, PROBLEMS AND PENALTIES

Getting married a second time is *not* a very private affair. Complications surrounding a second marriage seem to come as a shock to those involved in the situation. Just about every person I know who has gone through a second marriage experience has commented on the paradoxes, has bemoaned the problems and has wrestled with the penalties imposed by the legal system and the pressures resulting from the cultural mores and attitudes.

Apparently people enjoy speculating on marriage choice and enjoy commenting on impending marriages; they speculate on the motivations of participants and predict the outcomes. Recently, this fact was made clear when an older man married a younger girl. The middle-aged men in the community guessed that "he probably has a pot full of money," while their female counterparts commented that "it's better to be an old man's darling than a young man's slave!" Both men and women hinted that the marriage probably wouldn't last, and if it did last, the woman wouldn't be faithful. The implication was, of course, that the man married for sex and the woman married for money, and that those reasons for the marriage were not enough to maintain it!

1

"Getting married a second time is not a very private affair."

> *To meet approval, one's public behavior must be fairly consistent with idealized cultural values. Idealized values are quite different from real values.*

Of course, these comments and attitudes are themselves social pressures which will affect a relationship and add problems to an already strained situation. Any action which goes against socially acceptable public behavior will meet such pressure. I make a distinction between public behavior and private behavior of individuals. To meet approval, one's public behavior must be fairly consistent with **idealized** cultural values. Idealized values are quite different from **real** values. Idealized values are those which society pretends exist. A good example of differences between real and idealized values is apparent in almost any community and two cases will help to illustrate these differences.

The first case is Timothy S. and Carol. This couple has been married for twenty-five years. They have raised successful children and are respected in the small southern community where they have always lived. Carol attends church regularly and Timothy attends occasionally. Timothy makes a good living and "provides well for his **family**." Tim's wife is a good mother *Timothy S. Carol* and looks after the family's welfare. Timothy has a lover (who rents a home and land from him) and together they have produced two children. This illegitimate family is basically dependent upon Timothy for survival and he keeps them in a fashion higher than most of the other people in their socio-economic (lower class) situation.

Everyone in the community has heard about Timothy's extramarital affair and occasionally whispers are heard about it. But Timothy has not been censored publicly because certain idealized values were met. He has avoided severe pressure because of the following:

1. He does not make any public announcement about the illegitimate family he has fathered; he (and the community) pretends it did not exist.

2. He provides well for his legitimate family and they present an image of a stable family in their community.

3

3. The illegitimate family is better off and the legitimate family is no worse off as a result of Tim's behavior. Of course, the illegitimate family is of a lower socio-economic level and generally accepted in the community is the fact that they are essentially "property"—to be looked after and used.

Since the community accepts a double standard for men ("real" value), Timothy's behavior is not seen as deviating from the respectable norm. The only deviation of different behavior is the wife's acceptance of the situation. However, Carol can easily ignore the other family since Timothy has not embarrassed her by any public display of his lover and their illegitimate children.

The second case is Johnny F. and Irene. This couple had been married for twenty-five years and they, too, have reared successful children. One child has completed high school **Johnny F.**
with honors and is now in college, and the other two child- **Irene**
ren are working. Johnny and Irene have little in common so
the family has been held together basically for the "sake of the children."

Johnny and Irene did few things together as a couple. They both attended church and both worked. Johnny is a good provider, has his own retail business and holds a minor political office in town. To the community, Irene and Johnny appear to be an "ideal" family.

After the children left home, Johnny, having some extra time and money, joined a sports club and became involved in hunting, fishing and boating. Irene did not object to these hobbies, but did not want to participate. Basically, she wanted her free time to play bridge with her friends and visit with her parents.

Johnny met an attractive female club member, Valeria "Mac." They enjoyed every moment together. Johnny and "Mac" seemed
to have the same sense of humor, similar values, and they **Johnny F.**
viewed the world from a common frame of reference. They **"Mac"**
wanted to be together for the rest of their lives, and they **Irene**
wanted the world to know how they felt about each other.
They felt that their love and their choices would hurt no one. For all practical purposes, Johnny and Irene were living separate lives, and "Mac" had been divorced for several years. With naivete, they announced their love. Johnny and "Mac" told their friends that Johnny intended to get a divorce so they could be married. Johnny told Irene of his love for "Mac," expecting her to accept and understand his need to share his life with

4

this new person whom he loved. Johnny explained to Irene that they had, after all, put on a facade for the sake of the children, and that a divorce would be natural. Divorce would also be an honest acknowledgement of the existing relationship, he argued.

Irene was furious. She would not accept a divorce. She informed Johnny that she had "given him the best years of her life." She pleaded with him to "have his fling and then come home!" She threatened him with a legal suit and attempted to alienate their children, their friends, their pastor and church members.

In the community, Irene is depicted as the abused, used and help-less female. "Mac" is, of course, depicted by Irene and the community as the "other woman." Johnny's family and friends urged him to return home, to "act sensibly," to have his fling while he was going through his middle-aged crisis and then settle down to "his place."

Church members were polite but cool. A flurry of invitations arrived to *Johnny and Irene* for dinners, dances and trips. These invitations came mostly from friends and family. However, as Johnny persisted in his resolution to obtain a divorce and marry "Mac," friends and family support began to slip away. Pressure was exerted on him to resign his seat on the city council. He was replaced as a trustee for the church. His credit at the local bank was questioned. "Mac" received threatening and obscene phone calls. Johnny lost business in the community in which he had worked for years. Even after Johnny and "Mac" were married, "Mac" was not accepted as his wife by many of his friends. One of the older church members always referred to Irene as "Johnny's real wife," and to "Mac" as "that woman he's living with."

Society is not so interested in having individuals uphold the real values of the culture or to conform to the legal aspects of marriage and sexual relationships as much as they are in having individuals accept and teach (or uphold) the idealized cultural values of society.

These two cases are somewhat extreme, but they represent the positions encountered in society. Persons caught up in legal battles and social hassles of divorce and remarriage are confronted with these discrepancies. These individuals have to resolve this reality in a manner similar to the adolescent attempting to establish his identity as an adult. Part of the problem is traceable to the insecurity of the individual and part to the ambivalence of society. The confrontation with societal values gives rise to the frequent comment, "I just don't believe it!"

Individuals realize that society seems threatened by their behavior, but they do not know why. Usually the person feels unfairly punished, as though society publishes one set of rules and yet plays by another set! I believe that "cultural schizophrenia" about sex, divorce and second marriage is a result of a prevailing belief that to condone sexual deviation from the idealized norm or the reality of divorce make one's own marriage vulnerable. People believe they have to control the behavior of others in order to protect themselves.

The two preceding cases illustrate the attitudes of society and they also illustrate the first statement in this Chapter, that is, that getting married a second time is **not** a very private affair. Age and maturity, or knowing one's own mind, is not the criterion for society's approval. Divorce statistics, along with the statistics concerning crime and mental illness, are given to validate the notion that society has failed to inculcate moral standards and that the outlook for the future is bleak indeed. Seldom do we see any reference to the number of happy and unhappy marriages—the quality of the marriage relationship. Many satisfying marriages exist, but great percentages of these good marriages are second ones for one or both partners. This fact is true in spite of the social pressures a second marriage must endure.

Sometimes a second marriage is successful for awhile, but the couple does not maintain the initial relationship. One woman who has lived a productive, exciting life explained that she had three successful marriages and three successful divorces. She told me that as she changed and developed, she met and fell in love with three wonderful men who shared her life (for as long as they were compatible). She and her husbands had broad interests and busy lives. She felt it was reasonable that their relationships ended as they pursued their different goals. She insisted that each marriage was successful for as long as it lasted, and that the divorces were successful because they were accomplished with amicable good will and grace. She said she wishes that everyone could be as fortunate in love as she. She feels she is richer from each of these satisfying intimate relationships.

Truly when people change, marriage changes and sometimes dissolves. What people have failed to realize—to take into account— is the fact that people should change. If two people get married as youths, the probability is great that they will not continue to develop and change in a similar fashion. The probability is that they will grow apart. They will literally be different people from the two who got married. This

6

fact does not mean that the marriage should not have taken place. A bitter father remarked recently, "Our second daughter worked to send her husband through law school, and now he doesn't think she's good enough for him. They're getting a divorce!" What the father failed to realize is that they both have changed, in different ways, and the point is likely that neither can accommodate the needs of the other. In the view of the father, one partner had to be "right" and the other had to be "wrong." The father reflects the cultural attitude that one partner is the wronged and the other the perpetrator of some evil intention.

When a marriage fails both have changed, in different ways, and neither may accommodate the needs of the other. However, the tendency in society is to make one partner right and the other partner wrong.

Another change which has affected our traditional marriage patterns and expectations is a change in society. We have moved to a technological society. When we were mostly a nation of farmers, a mother, a father and children were all needed to maintain the self-sufficient family unit. The division of labor was clear and the role of each member was important to produce, preserve and utilize the basic ingredients for survival. In an industrial society, the family is no longer a self-sufficient unit; the division of labor is not clear cut. Societal changes bring about human value changes and role identification and expectations become blurred and unclear. Under this technological system the family is no longer needed solely to meet survival needs; the family stays together now because the unit meets emotional needs. Yet we have done little to educate our society to meet emotional needs. We still impart "traditional" values (e.g., the woman will be a wife and mother; the man will be a provider and father). We have overlooked or ignored the fact that the world has indeed changed! More is expected of marriage partners than that they come together to produce one or more offspring. Even the expectation that married couples will have children is changing. The couple now has the right (and the option) to decide if they wish to be parents, and if they do, when the event will happen and how many children they will have. This gives the couple and each partner individually a great deal of flexibility in their lives.

Longevity is another factor which is coming to the fore and influencing the stability of marriage and expectations of living together as husband and wife "until death do us part." In earlier times, when one took a marriage partner, the prime of life was well over by the time the last of the children left home. As a matter of fact, in earlier times, a general rule was for one of the children to remain unmarried and at home to care for the "aged" parents. Now, when parents have completed the task of parenting (rearing their children) and have seen their last child successfully through school and into college or work, they are often just reaching the peak of their physical well being. These couples are still mobile upward in their occupation. "Until death" from this point, is equal to the years they have already lived! If their child-rearing years have been happy and satisfying, the couple can continue to set new goals, establish new priorities and move toward new and better experiences—together. But if their lives have been a burden for either, or both, then for the couple to set goals together is very difficult. If they have not participated in a wide range of common activities, they will find difficult, or impossible, viewing the world from the same perceptual field and they will continue to grow (or drift) apart. Like Johnny and Irene, they will have fewer common concerns until they have nothing left. Social pressures relating to "till death do us part" will not be sufficient to hold the marriage together. Participants in the present-day marriage feel they deserve more out of the relationship than a feeling of obligation and responsibility.

Longevity—life together after the kids.

Society's attitudes and teachings are contradictory. For example, we tend to assume that children of divorced parents have more problems than children whose parents are together. We seldom look at the quality of the relationship as long as it's "respectable." Divorced parents are blamed for creating far more problems than are fathers or mothers who are absent from home for other reasons. To hear that a child's problems are the result of parent's divorce is not unusual, but we seldom hear a child's behavior blamed on a father who is missing in action or fighting a war or dead. We list divorce as a statistic that represents our nation's moral failures, and at the individual level, we force an attitude of the "blameless" and the "blamed." While divorce is condoned as a legal solution to a problem and even by most churches as a valid resolution of a disintegrated marriage contract, somehow the fact is not recognized or dealt with on the personal level as one alternative solution to problems between the partners. When marriage ends in divorce, the general belief is that the marriage was a mistake from the beginning and should not have happened.

Marriage, divorce and remarriages are laden with cultural values and traditions and cannot be understood solely in terms of our religious or legal system.

Marriage, divorce and remarriages are laden with cultural values and traditions and cannot be understood solely in terms of our religious or legal system. As individuals expand their contacts and their personal and financial influence, they multiply the extent and importance of these undefined but real values and traditions. So a second marriage, coming later in life and involving extended family relationships and affecting more "other" people, actually becomes a very public affair. This public interest and involvement may baffle the couple who is intent on a private marriage! Unexpected reactions of family and friends are not conducive to continuing established friendships, and reestablishing a system involving old friendships in the new marriage is difficult. Relationships are strained at a very time when the concerns of the couple need attention. The new marriage relationship must take priority for the couple if the marriage is to succeed. During this tense and difficult time, for feelings to be hurt and the once meaningful relationships to be destroyed, never to be rebuilt, is not unusual. The situation is like a tug-of-war for attention and assurances. Too many people want too much all at once. Old friends and family members want assurance that their places have not altered (and of course, they have—somewhat); and new marriage partners and their relationships want assurances that they are important and a part of the system (and of course the system has not developed to accommodate these demands).

Some of these frustrations and tensions were expressed by Alfred M. when he described what happened when he announced his intentions to marry Alicia. Alfred, a popular widower, fully expected his numerous friends to be delighted with his lovely fian- **Alfred** cee and thought that they would be even more delighted **Alicia** that he had found a perfect mother for his two young sons. The children liked her and she liked them. Alfred was sure that he and Alicia would be happy together and that working together they could establish a new and complete family.

Alfred's wife had been dead for three years, but he, with the help of a live-in maid, had kept the family together. Through these years he had suffered the pangs of loneliness and the frustrations of being an only parent to the boys. His own family, his in-laws and his friends paid frequent visits to his home, and the children were invited out frequently. Alfred was included in social events of the community and was presented at these affairs as **the most** eligible bachelor in the community—a "good catch." If Alfred hinted he would prefer not to be thrown with some unattached female, or that he would prefer to choose his own companions, he was assured by his friends that they were "concerned for his own happiness" and that they were "trying to help." He was encouraged to find a "nice girl who would be a good mother for the **poor** boys" (they were always referred at as **poor** boys—even though they seemed happy enough and their needs were being met quite adequately). Alfred needed a female companion far more than they needed a mother. But with good grace he accepted these intrusions into his life and even admitted he was flattered and pleased with their concern and involvement.

When Alfred first met Alicia she had just moved into his community. She was in the final process of her divorce. Her twenty-year marriage to Ron had been confining in terms of enjoyment of life and limiting in terms of her own growth and development. Only after her last child had finished high school, did she dare express   **Alicia** her feelings about the marriage and pursue her desire for   **Ron** new and different experiences. Her husband agreed to the divorce, but set about immediately to paint her in the public's mind as a terrible person who had done great wrong and had brought sorrow and shame upon him.

Alicia had assumed the divorce would be a private decision involving herself and her husband primarily, and their children to a lesser extent. However, her husband created so much talk and brought about so much criticism of her, she felt she could not continue to live in that community. She had found little support from her own family and her friends, so she had moved to Alfred's hometown to work and live.

As mentioned earlier, when a marriage ends, people look for someone to blame. In this instance, Alicia was the "bad guy" and her husband, Ron, the "good guy." Since Ron enjoyed sympathy and was the center of attention, he basked in the limelight that was his throughout the divorce proceedings. He shared and amplified details of their agreements and disagreements—who said what to whom. This behavior had oppressed Alicia and made her want to be free of the marriage. She wanted new experiences and he wanted only to limit the world's interest to focus on himself.

Alicia was bright, a competent medical technician, and rather self-sufficient. She had never felt she belonged in the life style she shared with Ron, but since she did not know how to bring about a change and stay in the marriage, she chose to end it. She was willing and able to develop a new life style that included new people and new activities. She longed to be a part of that world which she dreamed existed during those years she was confined to her role as Ron's wife.

Alfred brought new excitement to Alicia, and she was to him like a ray of hope—a second chance. They were unbelievably happy to find each other. Alicia and the boys developed an immediate rapport and a quick friendship. She was firm and consistent with them, and they responded with trust and delight. The loneliness which Alfred had felt turned to longing and his frustrations turned to delight in their shared parenting responsibility. Alicia approached each day with happy anticipation and a recognition that she had made an altogether satisfying choice. Evidence was that theirs would be a happy and enduring relationship, and that everyone—they and the children—would benefit from the marriage partnership.

To Alfred, his friends and relatives reacted in quite a surprising manner. Thinking he was sufficiently mature to know his own mind and his own needs, Alfred could not believe the negative reactions he received. Numerous attempts were made to discredit Alicia. His friends asked him if he was **sure** he was doing the right thing—especially for the children. "There's no fool like an old fool," said a relative when she was convinced that Alfred planned to marry Alicia. People even tried to alienate the children—to set up a "cruel stepmother" image. Alfred and Alicia were determined to be together, but they would have preferred to do so with the blessings of the community. The blessings of their friends would have eased their adjustment and helped them find their place in the community. Having support rather than hostility, from families, friends and Alfred's in-laws would have made easier the establishment of an open and trusting family atmosphere. They had hoped to include the important people in Alfred's and the children's lives in their family and friendship circle, but various reactions made this impossible.

The purpose of negative reaction is not easy to comprehend. Different individuals and groups probably reacted negatively for different reasons. Some motivation for adverse behavior is typical of that found in any criticism. These criticisms are as follows:

1. Certain individuals lost their places (i.e., their importance) in the lives of one or more of the people involved. Thus, these individuals resented the intrusion of an "outsider" into their own lives.

2. Certain people needed someone to "see after," and wanted to continue the "helping-the-'poor'-children" role. In a sense, these people enjoy being martyrs, and feel they are important only when they are helping.

3. A few people were self-righteous and some honestly thought the marriage was morally wrong because Alicia had been divorced, and worse still, she had been the one to initiate the divorce. These people hold a " 'till death do us part" attitude and believe marriages are made in heaven. Mostly from this group the children heard negative references to the stepmother relationship. Some people actually believed that Alicia could not possibly love this new family as she could "love her own." People could never comprehend that the stepchildren became, indeed, her own.

4. Jealousy was a real motivation for much criticism. A good number of females had hoped to marry Alfred and they were, of course, unhappy. Some couples were jealous that Alicia and Alfred seemed to be so happy and had a new start and a "second chance" while they were stuck in a mundane or unhappy marriage. Some persons were jealous that a woman who already seemed to have everything was getting more—a husband and children—and some thought that a man whose wife had died should marry someone who could serve as a "replacement" for the services provided by a wife and mother, that is, as a convenience, and not for love and happiness.

5. For some, the situation was just a topic of conversation with little concern except to socialize. Since many seem to dwell on the problems of the world as opposed to the positive aspects, naturally they sounded negative. Also, the chance existed that if the marriage didn't prove satisfactory, individuals could say they

had predicted failure! If the marriage was a success, no one would remember their gloomy predictions. The situation is somewhat like the obstetrician who confided that he always tells the prospective parents that he predicts their child will be a girl. He says that if the baby is a boy, the parents are so happy that they forget his prediction; if the child is a girl, they think he was very clever.

These examples are some of the paradoxes of second marriages. But they are also paradoxes of life. We interact with others in terms of our own agenda as well as what seems appropriate to the situation.

A second marriage brings together the forces of more relationships than does a first marriage, and as the number of participants increases, interactions multiply and clear communication becomes more difficult. For instance, when only two people are involved, communication is a two-way process as shown in Figure 1.1.

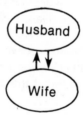

Figure 1.1. Husband and Wife Communication Involves Two People.

In Figure 1.2 is shown the complexity of the situation when three people are involved in the group, and in Figure 1.3 is illustrated the multiplying effect of interactions with four individuals. The complexity is tremendous as these individuals (parts of the family system) are increased.

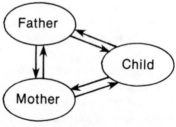

Figure 1.2. Group Interactions For Three Individuals.

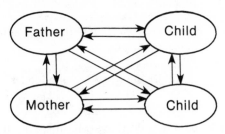

Figure 1.3. Group Interactions for Four Individuals.

In second marriages, adults and the children of these adults are most directly involved. But so, too, are in-laws, friends, colleagues and business associates. All of these other people bring their expectations to the new relationship. If the expectations of all were met, marriage would create a system revolving around two people, that is, new marriage partners. If expectations are not met and the marriage is *not* accepted, the marriage represents two systems held together by one common point, the couple. Conceptually, this latter type of system would look something like that depicted in Figure 1.4.

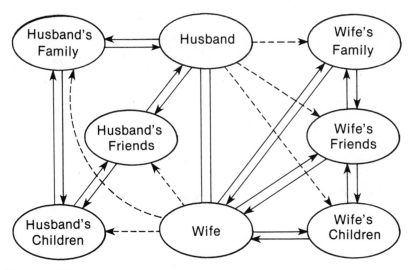

Figure 1.4. Expectations of Interactions of Second Marriages Which Meet With Disapproval.

A great deal of effort, determination and resolution is needed to bring about a functioning new family system where everyone is important in that new system. This new functioning requires that all the individuals agree upon certain ideas:

1. The person or persons to be included (each person must be included).

2. The individual or individuals will interact with whom (no "mine-yours-and-ours" attitude—if the new family is to be stable and satisfying).

3. The values that are important and the goals that are to be set.

Conceptually, a solid new family-interaction system would be quite different from that shown in Figure 1.4. Instead, the parts would interact in the fashion depicted in Figure 1.5.

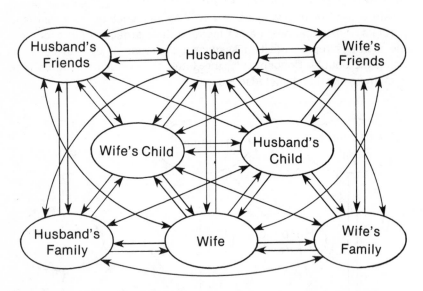

Figure 1.5. Conceptual System of Interaction When All Parts Are Important.

Developing a healthy-functioning family system with a new marriage partner is not easy and requires studied attention and effort.

Maintaining an old family system even when it is dysfunctional and unhealthy is easier than developing new ways of relating and responding. Dysfunctional patterns established in the first marriage and family tend to be carried over into the second marriage and family system. Both partners must work at a marriage and care about the outcomes to really succeed. To see an individual marry a second time a person with the same type of problems and behavior pathology that was obvious in the first marriage is not unusual. For example, the woman with an alcoholic husband will marry an alcoholic the second time around, and the man with a clinging vine wife about whom he constantly complained will marry another clinging vine. Part of the explanation for this lies in the fact that they know how to relate to this type of problem personality, and part of the situation is that their way of relating reinforces those unhealthy responses. Behavior patterns are established quickly.

Joe and Joan had been married several months. Joan said to Joe, "Joe, I wish you would tell David. . ." (David is his son by **Joe** a first marriage). Joe responded firmly and appropriately, **Joan** "If you want David to know this, you should tell him!" **David**

Two people who respect each other and have set a goal of developing a healthy family from new members brought together in a new marriage relationship will assist each other in developing clear and appropriate interaction patterns.

Two people who respect each other and have set a goal of developing a healthy family from new members brought together in a new marriage relationship will assist each other in developing clear and appropriate interaction patterns. If Joan had succeeded in communicating her disapproval of David's behavior through the father, this would have been a first step in setting up a pattern of behavior (rules for the family) which looked something like the pattern depicted in Figure 1.6.

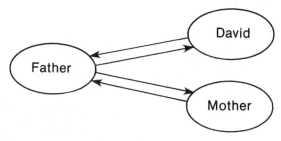

Figure 1.6. Mother Communicates Through Father.

Joan insists that the reason she referred the behavior to Joe was because David was a boy and not because he happened to be her stepson, but that really does not make any difference. The problem is the same in either instance. The important factor is that communication be direct and clear with as few hidden motivations as possible. If Joan

speaks directly to David, she has to deal with her feelings and David's feelings. No possibility exists that she will use her disapproval of David's behavior to punish Joe, or for David to feel he has to please Joan in order to keep the respect of his father. Only when we interact with our family members in a fashion as illustrated in Figure 1.7 do we communicate to them that we respect them as individuals and accept them as unique and important in their own right. No one gets "used" in this healthy inter-actional system.

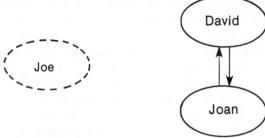

Figure 1.7. Direct Communication.

New responses or ways of behaving require that the individual make a studied effort to change from the usual pattern. Like changing any habit, this produces some degree of discomfort. To get an idea of the discomfort and problems involved in behaving differently, try the following experiment:

> In the morning change your usual way of dressing. If you usually put on your left shoe first, put on the right one first. If you usually have coffee before dressing, dress first, and so forth.

If one is to relate successfully to a new marriage partner, one will have to accommodate the new person. To change all or most of the unhealthy interactions is a must; to change all or most of the behavior which annoys the other or conflicts with the other's pattern of behavior is also crucial. For the older couple in a second marriage the first few months or even years may be quite painful, and usually one or both members feel that they have had to give up "quite a bit" for this new life style.

The cases of Timothy and Carol and Johnny and Irene are examined again to illustrate the kind of behavior patterns which are developed and maintained over time because they become comfortable. As you will recall, Timothy has an illegitimate family. He perceives women as "good" and "bad." He sees the "good" woman as married to a man who respects her—and he calls being provided for and not embarrassed as respected—and he believes Carol is happy if she has a home and children. He also believes he, as a man, has a right to enjoy sex with a "bad" woman, and that this woman enjoys sex and her man, and her home and children are of little

Timothy
Carol

importance to her. The women react to his behavior in such a fashion as to reinforce his belief. The situation works for him and he is comfortable relating to both women on this level.

Assume that Timothy enters a new marriage. We would predict he would again choose a marriage partner who expects little from the husband except a home and children. He could not tolerate a "liberated" woman who accepts marriage as a partnership and sex as part of that relationship to be enjoyed by both partners. He would not be able to relate sexually to a "good" woman in the same manner he does a "bad" woman. He would believe that if his wife enjoyed sex she was not a good woman.

Similarly, Carol is quite comfortable with her "door mat" role. She expects to be a servant to husband and children and justified her existence in the world as a "good wife and mother." She also believes that if she is patient and good that her husband will change his ways and in the religious sense, "be saved." Therefore, she will not speak out or stand up about her beliefs. If she should marry again she would maintain this posture. She would not and could not maintain a fifty-fifty partnership because she also thinks a "good" man is one who is the head of the household, and a "good" woman is one who stands by her man.

In contrast to these two individuals, Johnny and Irene are both rather wholesome and independent individuals. Nevertheless, they habitually function independently and with little input from each other. Assume that they marry again. Involving **Johnny** a new partner (wife) in his decision making would be **Irene** difficult for Johnny. For him to decide for himself because he wants the successes and failures to be his is quite comfortable. For him to trust another's judgment—even Mac's is hard.

Irene is more or less accustomed to having her own life to herself, but at the same time having her physical or survival needs met by her husband. She does not like to be involved in family decision making. She prefers someone else to be responsible for the successes and failures. If she should marry again and be forced into a position of a fifty-fifty relationship, or in a situation where she had to manage the family resources, she would have great difficulties adjusting. She would feel the world was unfair. She is unprepared to confront life. When possible, she avoids making choices.

Giving up familiar patterns of behaving creates new problems and most people do so with reluctance. Trying new behavior **Robert** means facing the unfamiliar and unpredictable. This is also **Rachael** difficult and threatening. Some, like Robert, ignore the need for change.

Robert and Rachael are to be married—a second marriage for both. Robert has had great reluctance in meeting Rachael's children and other relatives, and she has not even met his children. He says that since one is an adult and married with a home of her own that his marriage to Rachael does not concern this daughter. His other daughter will live with his former wife. He does not understand why Rachael mentions the situation so often and has made an issue of it.

Actually, Robert likes to keep his life compartmentalized. He perceives himself as the center of any relationship. He does not want to share his position or to make the parts into an integrated system. He is more comfortable to have his life divided into segments. His life is basically handled on a person-to-person dimension as shown in Figure 1.8. He even relates to his father and mother in this manner. Rachael, on the other hand, thrives on an environment with many stimuli. She sought professional help because she could not understand why Robert should feel left out when others were around, and she could not understand why he did not involve her in his relationships with his family and friends.

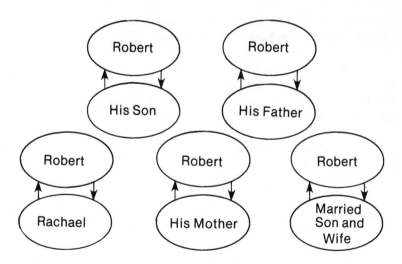

Figure 1.8. Robert's Relationships Are One Dimensional.

While she now understands the dynamics of his behavior, she has been unsuccessful in working with Robert to resolve their problems. Of course Robert does not see that he has a problem since he is perfectly happy with Rachael. He does not even understand what Rachael is talking about when she tried to discuss the situation. If Robert and Rachael marry without resolving the situation Rachael will probably be forced to limit her contacts with her family and friends to those times when Robert is not with her. She can also expect him to pursue independent relationships, and he will not generally involve her in activities such as his hobbies, business and recreation.

To learn to share life space with more than one person at a time will be very difficult for Robert. Unless he really wants to bring about this change in his life, he will not do so. At this time, he does not recognize that his way of relating will be a problem in his proposed marriage. As a child Robert was the center of interest. He was treated as special and he still views the world from this attitude.

For an individual to be so reluctant to meet prospective in-laws and other relatives is somewhat unusual. Most likely the in-laws are reluctant to meet the prospective spouse and recognize the impending marriage. Also, for some families to incorporate the children that may be involved in the second marriage and to accept them as having an equal place in the family structure and system is quite difficult. Family systems are sometimes highly resistant to change. New members can cause resentment and stress between the family members. The dynamics of an inflexible family system are illustrated below.

Assume you have a functioning family system made up of a father, mother, six-year-old granddaughter and daughter (divorced). These members relate in such a way that their behavior indicates that the family has certain rules. That is, they believe the following:

1. Father (or grandfather) is the major decision-maker.

2. The grandchild is the most important person to be considered.

3. Mother (and grandmothers) are to be protected from the problems of the world (father knows best).

Now let us assume the daughter marries again, and her new husband has a three-year-old son. The members of the family system are drastically changed and so are the rules which govern their behavior.

The husband and son bring their own rules of behavior to the new family. Assume that the expectations of the husband are that (a) he will be the major decision-maker, and, (b) boys are little men and girls are to be looked after.

While husband and grandfather hold the same general attitudes about male-female relationships, they will be in opposition in terms of their own roles. The grandfather will lose his place with his daughter as her husband assumes that place. The grandchildren will have to share their positions with the grandparents, and the granddaughter's favored position will be uprooted. The husband will meet unexpected demands from his new stepdaughter, who will resent being upstaged by her young brother, and the son will have to share his favored position with his new sister.

If the individuals are unaware of the dynamics of the situation, they will probably feel hurt and unloved and they will look at the new members as "causing" the problems. Since everyone involved does not realize the impact of what is happening, they think the other person is wrong and each individual will attempt to cut-off contact with these new people. All the family members can resolve the situation only through open communication, accepting the changing family composition as forcing a changing of roles of the participants, that is, the **rules** in the family, and wanting to understand and accommodate these new experiences.

A healthy family is flexible and can accommodate change. We have all seen families all but destroyed when a family member was removed by divorce or death, or even temporarily absent because of school or war. We have also seen families destroyed when new members were added: a new marriage partner, a new child, an elderly parent, and so forth. We have seen children unable to leave home, or to stay away for any reasonable length of time if they were forced by circumstances to leave home. These inflexible families have a rigid set of rules. They have definite expectations for each individual in the system and the rules are such that the individuals are limited to certain behaviors. These are the families we see in crisis. These are families which need some external person to work with them to help bring about some new rules—to open the system—to try out some new behaviors. These families produce children who expect people to behave as they believe they should, and members of these rigid families attempt to control the behavior of others. When these children are in situations where they cannot control the other people, they feel unfairly treated, are frustrated and tend to withdraw.

Most of the problems of a second marriage are human relations problems. New relationships make underlying problems obvious. With the restructuring of the family, personality problems seem to surface. When interactions with the systems are disrupted, new expectations have to be accommodated. Marriage is not a panacea for unhealthy and unfulfilling relationships. Marriage does offer an excellent opportunity for the family to focus on working out their communication and relationship problems.

I have talked about the paradoxes inherent in second marriage relationships and I have raised some of the problems of developing a new family system. I could also categorize some of the problems as penalties; penalties imposed on people who make a decision to marry again.

The penalties basically revolve around financial and legal problems and responsibilities. A few have to do with the judgmental and unaccepting nature of fellow beings.

Society's legal system reflects, to a great extent, the middle-class values of the culture. The middle-class value holds the man responsible for the financial welfare of the family and the female responsible for the psychological welfare of the family. Therefore, when a marriage dissolves, still the general rule is that the man must continue to provide for the well-being of his former wife and children, and the woman must continue to maintain a home for the children. Of course, these attitudes are slowly changing, but this rule is still the expected. To the degree that individuals are hampered by the legal system (and social pressures also) to work out arrangements which are most satisfactory to all concerned, the second marriage for these individuals will be saddled with constraints imposed by the courts. These constraints limit the degree of freedom of the second marriage partners.

Just as surely as certain responsibilities for former marriages are placed upon individuals, the new marriage is entered into with a similar set of responsibilities. If a man, for example, has most of his resources tied up in the support of a former wife and/or children, he is still expected to provide for his family when he marries again. The situation is often totally impossible, but relief is usually not forthcoming. A couple facing such circumstances should discuss the meaning these problems can have on their own relationship. They should not underplay the importance of financial pressures on thier own ability to adjust to each other and to develop a satisfactory life style. The unique set of problems, pressures and penalties may mean that the wife must work and they may not be able to afford the luxury of having children together.

Apparently individuals who are now in the over-thirty age bracket have stayed in an unsatisfactory marriage until an external reason existed for getting out. That is, the pressure of a bad marriage was not enough to bring about a divorce. Therefore, most of these over-thirty people who divorced did so because one of the partners met another person with whom he/she related on a more satisfying level and whom he/she wished to marry. On the other hand, seemingly for the under-thirty age group an unsatisfactory marriage itself is sufficient reason for a divorce. These young people feel that life has more to offer than having to share a life style with an individual who meets few of their psychological needs. Therefore, the younger individuals tend to get a divorce and then to initiate a search for another long-term relationship (which may or may not include marriage) with someone of the opposite sex.

Both of these situations create their own sets of problems. For the individual seeking a divorce to marry another, the problems usually involve the following:

1. resistance from the spouse;

2. legal entanglements which will prove costly;

3. severe social pressure which may take its toll on the profession-al advancement or occupation of the individuals involved; and

4. feelings of guilt for having involved other people in a problem which is personal in nature and has gone unresolved for so long.

For the individual divorcing and then seeking a new meaningful relationship, the problems usually involve the following:

1. frustrations and confusions concerning what went wrong and how to predict a more stable relationship;

2. resentment and a feeling of unfulfilled promises or incompleted tasks because the marriage was terminated for what is often per-ceived as a less than satisfactory reason;

3. a lack of self-identity and clear life-style goals; and

4. a cynical attitude toward long-term commitments and trust.

Paradoxes, problems and penalties are not unique to second marriages, but they do tend to be magnified in the second marriage relationship. In the first place, social pressures are more intense. To discard old ways of relating is difficult, even if those ways are dysfunctional and self defeating. New behavior patterns are always uncomfortable and effort is needed to establish a mutually satisfying relationship—with friend or spouse. And finally, a person brings a set of expectations, feelings and attitudes to a new marriage which may be quite different from those of the other individuals involved. These expectations are influenced by their past experiences and how they feel about them. The healthy-functioning individual will not back away from this new marriage relationship, but will use this second marriage as an opportunity to develop and grow—to create a new and better system where each individual will find a place that is satisfying. A healthy family produces happy healthy individuals. A second marriage is a second chance to develop such a family constellation.

ACTIVITIES FOR INDIVIDUALS AND FAMILIES

To Be Completed Following Reading of Chapter 1

Topic A—IDENTIFYING INDIVIDUAL/FAMILY VALUES

Activity 1.1. Briefly describe three incidents which occured lately which made you feel *good.* Then following each incident identify what about the incident made you feel good. (If this is a family activity each individual should work independently.)

Example: Incident— I sold some used books for more than I paid for

them.

Feeling— Selling the books for more than I paid for them

made me feel "clever" to make money.

a. Incident _____

_____

_____

Feeling _____

_____

_____

b. Incident _____

_____

_____

Feeling _____

_____

_____

c. Incident _____

_____

_____

Feeling _____

_____

_____

Activity 1.2. Using the information in Activity 1.1, complete the following sentence about yourself.

I feel good when _____

_____

_____

Activity 1.3. After having completed Activities 1.1 and 1.2, have a family discussion where members of the family share what makes them feel good. Together they can identify those values they have in common. Parents may want to help children identify positive ways to express their individual values. Information derived from Activities 1.1, 1.2, 1.3 will be useful in establishing family goals.

Topic B—FAMILY GOAL SETTING

Activity 1.4. Using the following outline, the family working as a group is to set a short-term goal. Every member of the family is to agree that the goal is important.
a. What short-term goal does the family wish to achieve?

_____

_____

b. How soon can the family achieve this goal (be realistic)?

_____

28

c. What values, individually and as a group, led to the choice of this goal?

Individual A: _____

Individual B: _____

Individual C: _____

Individual D: _____

Family as a Group: _____

d. What strengths, individually and as a group, does the family possess which will help to reach the goal?

Individual A: _____

Individual B: _____

Individual C: _____

Individual D: _____

Family as a Group: _____

e. What problems (barriers or situations) might occur which could hinder the achievement of the short-term goal?

_____

_____

f. Suggest one to three ways individuals or the family might manage each of the problems listed.

_____

_____

_____

_____

g. What next steps need to be taken to achieve the short-term goal?

What To Do	How To Do It	When To Do It	Who is Responsible
1)_____	_____	_____	_____
_____	_____	_____	_____
2)_____	_____	_____	_____
_____	_____	_____	_____
3)_____	_____	_____	_____
_____	_____	_____	_____

h. When will the family again meet to determine progress toward achievement of the goal?

Date:_____Time:_____Place: _____

i. If modifications are made in the goal at the time of the meeting, write the modified goal statements in the space provided.

_____

_____

_____

CHAPTER 2

LIFE STYLING—A SECOND CHANCE

To some couples, life is a challenge; the world is a lovely place. Simply not enough time in a day is available to do all of the things these individuals who are alive, alert and excited want to do. Some couples have problems and enjoy solving them because they identify with success, growth, fun, love, being and becoming. To such couples their world expands year by year.

To other couples, life is threatening; the world is an awful place. Time drags on and the individuals are overly concerned about the future. These couples can hardly cope now and are fearful that they cannot cope in the years to come when age and health are factors with which to contend. Some couples are depressed, withdrawn and fearful. These individuals identify with failure, pain, unmet needs and defeat. For some couples their personal world becomes smaller and smaller, year by year, until their goals are limited and focused on survival problems. To these couples to wait for the inevitable end is their philosophy.

Walt and Addie are a couple who enjoy their world. Their marriage is a second marriage for both. Walt and Addie have had the usual financial worries of a couple maintaining two households with children from having divorced their previous spouses. Walt took twelve years and Addie ten years to reach the level of autonomy necessary to end their first unhappy marriages. Walt and Addie were the first individuals in their respective families to be divorced and pressures to stay married were intense. The changes this couple has made have been difficult and painful, but, at the same time, enlightening and satisfying. Both Walt and Addie are now in the life-styling process of their second marriage—and they appear to be successful. Both are growing and they believe this is good. Walt and Addie are planning together for their continuing growth and self development, are optimistic about tomorrow and are happy about today.

Walt

Addie

We will "work together to establish individual and partnership developmental goals."

Walt and Addie agreed before they were married that they would work together to establish individual and partnership developmental goals. Both individuals also agreed that the ultimate responsibility for growth and development would reside with the individual, so one could not blame the other if life proved to be dissatisfying. Walt and Addie had grown up in a culture which was not concerned about adult development. Generally, when people finished high school or got married and/or took a job, they were not expected to obtain additional skills or establish educational goals for personal development. Also, the adults in their home communities were "other" directed (sometimes referred to as externally controlled) and generally failed to accept responsibility for their own behavior. For example, Walt's brother, Busby, **Busby** and his wife, Jolyn, were externally controlled. Jolyn **Jolyn** blamed Busby for her weight problem. She was sixty pounds overweight, but said her overweight was because Busby was getting home late so often that it made her nervous, and when she was nervous she overate. She could not help herself. Busby argued that he was late because he lived so far from his work and that he could not move closer because Jolyn would not leave her hometown.

Walt and Addie have grown up playing those same psychological games. However, they learned about themselves and had changed. During the time Walt and Addie were trying to resolve problems in their first marriages, they had both received help. With counseling they had learned to **own** and **accept** their own behavior and their own feelings—and to express these feelings honestly and congruently. Now with their second marriage, they want to continue working on this new way of relating and being responsible. Thus their pact: to work together on common goals and common interests and to work separately on individual goals and individual interests.

Walt and Addie not only made such an agreement, but they also set up a plan by which they could accomplish their goals. They knew from experience that to want something was not enough: they had to develop a plan and implement the plan before their desires would be realized. "Things don't just happen" was Walt's way of expressing the situation.

Walt and Addie's plan calls for a brief time of uninterrupted discussion each day. They bring their thoughts, problems and successes to this discussion and they try to work out the details of solving problems together. The individual's responsibility is to offer problems or situations for discussion and to state these problems as clearly and accurately as possible. This process is their first step in maintaining an open and accepting attitude.

After the statement of the problem, the next step in the plan or process is for Walt and Addie to discuss alternative ways for solving the problem. They approach this part by listing all of the alternatives—even if the alternatives seem unrealistic or perhaps silly. Part of their plan is to generate ideas and not get stuck with the all-too-common belief that "there is no other way." Walt and Addie have heard that one too! When Busby and Jolyn have a problem, they seem to think of only one way to solve the problem, and if that way does not **Busby** work or is ineffective they are stuck with a bad solution. Busby and Jolyn do not realize that bad **procedure** causes their trouble. Busby and Jolyn are poor problem solvers because they do not generate ideas and find data which will help them find **Walt** good solutions. Walt is thankful that he has learned to go through the steps necessary for good problem solving. The first thing Walt learned about solving problems was to generate alternatives—and not to evaluate them until he had exhausted all ideas. Walt learned that if he does not evaluate the worth or goodness of the idea or alternative as he thinks of it he can think of more options. Walt found out that all problems have many possible solutions. He came to understand that a suicide note which said,". . . .this is the **only** way out" was believed by its author. Walt can now appreciate this point of view. While Walt knows that realistically many "ways out" exist for the individual who wrote the note, he also knows that the person saw no other way out of the problem. Walt realizes that at an earlier point in his own life he too was quite closed minded. He used to think of one alternative and then assume that it was the solution. Now he knows differently. Now he actually enjoys problem solving because he feels a certain creative power when he has a challenging problem to solve. Addie has had **Walt** many of the same types of experiences in her own life. So **Addie** Walt and Addie have an agreement to work out problems together in this systematic problem-solving fashion. This is another of those quiet joys they have learned to share.

Walt and Addie also enjoy testing the solutions they propose. Since neither Walt nor Addie wants to adhere to the traditional sex role stereotypes in their daily living activities, they have simply divided up their home maintenance work in a manner which is most agreeable to their individual work schedules, their interests and skills. They both assume responsibilities for getting certain things done and neither questions the other about that part of the plan nor interfers in the way tasks are approached. They are both trustful and trustworthy.

Amazingly Walt and Addie come near to achieving the goals they set. Life to them is exciting and a problem is a challenge, not an obstacle. When they fail, they use that failure as a learning experience. They don't blame each other for failure. When they succeed, they can enjoy their success.

Walt and Addie's individual development plan follows the same general pattern as their joint activities. Walt, though he's forty-one years old, is learning to fly. This is his most recent individual goal. If he is successful and if he buys part interest in a plane, Addie has agreed to take some lessons and see if she enjoys piloting also. At the present time, she is concentrating on Spanish. They are tentatively planning a month in Spain next year, and she wants to be able to speak the language. She has never taken a foreign language before.

Addie works. She and Walt share the household chores; their responsibilities are primarily based on interest and skill. Addie does most of the cooking—because she enjoys it—and Walt does most of the household cleaning and maintenance. They buy groceries together. Since so much money is spent to purchase groceries Walt and Addie feel that both should experience the problems of grocery buying and should know the food choices that are available.

Walt and Addie have a marriage partnership that is basically a fifty-fifty proposition. They are equals—compeers. Neither is responsible for the other but both are responsible for the relationship. They are not overly concerned about male-female roles. Together, they can accomplish far more than each can accomplish individually. This is synergism; that is, the production of the cooperative effort which is greater than the production of the two separate individuals.

The end goal is not so important to them as the process.

We can anticipate that Walt and Addie will continue to change. When they are much older, they will still be squeezing out every ounce of enjoyment from even the most mundane activity. The **end** goal is not so important to them as the **process**. This is their secret. I believe that a

35

marriage is no healthier or stronger than the least effective partner, and that the individual's deteriorating process begins when growth stops. Change is inevitable.

How different are Busby and Jolyn from Walt and Addie. As I indicated earlier, Busby and Jolyn are unable to define themselves as separate from each other. They have been married since high school—eighteen years. In those eighteen years **Busby** Busby and Jolyn have consciously sought few experi- **Jolyn** ences. Their basic motivation is for security, so they do the same thing over and over. They have the same few friends they always have had. They eat the same food they always have eaten. They go to the same church they went to as children. Busby makes the living and Jolyn keeps the house.

Jolyn is not well. She isn't sick, but she just never feels quite well. She is overweight by some sixty pounds, but she still feels hungry most of the time. Her home is well equipped and fairly new, so she doesn't have much to do. She has few hobbies, just cooking, sewing and church. She does not think that a working wife is proper. She has never learned to participate in new activities, and she sees most activities as appropriate for young people only. She spends a great deal of time just waiting and worrying. She leaves the important decisions to Busby and she does what he thinks is appropriate.

Busby is a good worker and values what others think of him. That he make sufficient wages to "care for" his wife, to maintain a nice home and to respect the conventions of the community is important to Busby. He spends his free time fishing or hunting with his best friends—or preparing for these activities. He and Jolyn visit their families almost weekly and attend church regularly. Busby and Jolyn have no children. Jolyn could never get pregnant even though the doctors could find no medical reason for her infertility. They have accepted the situation as God's will and anyway, at this point, they feel they are too old to be good parents. So they have stopped trying to have children. Actually, they seldom have sexual relations anymore. Jolyn waits for Busby to take the initiative and he is usually too preoccupied with his work or his fishing to be interested. Busby believes that sex is mostly a concern of youth and primarily of men, and he is somewhat relieved that his drives are no longer as urgent or intense as they once were. He believes something basically is sinful in sex and that the drive is something with which young boys must struggle to overcome. He also assumes that Jolyn has never enjoyed sex. He assumes few women do. Sometimes he wonders what Jolyn thinks about women's liberation and more specifically, what she thinks about the movies, press and television emphasis on women's sexual needs. He wonders if she is aware of the changing attitudes in this area, but he does not ask. The two just do not talk about "those kinds of things."

Sometimes Jolyn wishes she could express herself and let Busby know how she feels, but she says she was not "brought up" that way. She learned to be a good wife and to her a good wife is one who is subservient to her husband. "He makes the money," she says, "so he has a right to make the decisions." Busby is head of the household. Their marriage might be called a piggy-back relationship. Jolyn is defined as "the wife of Busby." She has little autonomy. She cannot do anything inappropriate to her perception of what a "wife" should be.

We can predict that Busby and Jolyn will become more and more fearful of life. We would predict that if Busby became disabled, they would have to go on welfare—or be supported by his or her family. Jolyn could not make a living. She would not be able to make decisions. Though they are still young in years, Busby and Jolyn are old in attitude. They have not set any new goals as adults, individually or together, and, thus, they have not experienced the joys and excitement of failure and/or success. Security is their basic motivation. Although they are seeking security, they are self-conscious and insecure. Because Busby and Jolyn cannot be totally assured of their world, they tend to do self-defeating things (such as over eating, over smoking, over working, etc.) to ease the pain of being! They can never know the sheer joy of *becoming* as long as they are afraid of *being.* They will not face life, recognize that change is inevitable and plan for change. Busby and Jolyn simply hide from this reality and wait for days to pass by without incident.

A second marriage, like a New Year, offers a psychological point when one seems to have a new beginning. This is an ideal time to initiate those changes which one would like to see take place. At the beginning of a second marriage is a good time to establish responsibility for one's own development and continuing growth. It is a good time for pushing out beyond the psychologically safe or "known" areas into the *Discomfort Zone,* that is, that area where change is possible because it is an area of new attempts and new behaviors. Learning means change and change always has some degree of discomfort. The degree to which a couple is willing to move into the *Discomfort Zone* is equal to their potential for change and thus their personal growth.

A new beginning is also a new time to anticipate the unexpected! With amazing regularity the same problems confront couples in the second marriage. Money, children, new relationships and conflict management are highly predictable problems. Less predictable, but surely a problem to be anticipated by many, are crises relating to aged parents, wills and inheritances, adult children and grandchildren and illness and death.

No taboo subjects should exist with the new partner. The most dangerous problem of all is the failure to communicate. Communication between partners is even more important for the second marriage than the first, especially if the first marriage ended by divorce. Apparently in a second marriage the couple is unprepared to confront areas of potential conflict because they were unable to resolve their problems with the first spouse. But problems are different. One does not build onto the old relationships. The new marriage is a total and discrete entity.

"They hear but don't listen."

In the first marriage, the problems relate most usually to immaturity, sexual incompatibility and lack of readiness for marriage. Youthful partners are likely to verbalize, but fail to communicate. They **hear** but don't **listen**. The maturity of the couple in the second marriage should be an asset in communication. With **Walt** practice, patience and desire, effective communication **Addie** skills can be learned. Walt and Addie are good examples of a mature couple who have learned the value of communication, goal setting and individual responsibility.

Our society teaches us to be concerned about what "they" will think if we do thus and so, or wear thus and so, even think thus and so. We learn what is proper for our age and station in life. Interestingly and paradoxically, the more effectively an individual buys into this attitude, the more difficult the process is to recognize one's own needs, to own one's behavior and to be open enough to share (the real) self with others—even the spouse. "Other" directed individuals are self-conscious. These individuals can never quite forget themselves and become totally involved in any activity because they are constantly evaluating the impact they are having on the other person. They are evaluating the evaluator!

Self-directed individuals, on the other hand, pay reasonable attention to the conventions of society because they know that conventions are the important fibers which hold the culture together. But having paid a reasonable respect to what others expect, self-directed individuals are able to move to what they want for themselves.

The self-directed person weighs or measures goodness in terms of his/her own values. Self-directed individuals can sort out for themselves what they want. Such individuals are not concerned overly about what others think. They are responsible to themselves and for themselves. If the self-directed individual's desires are contrary to the desires of others, then the individual is willing to suffer the loss of prestige to pursue his/her own goals. Self-directed individuals assume they have control over their own fate and within certain limitations and dimensions will exert that control. They are not afraid of their own humanness, so they can be open and sharing. They can say what they mean and mean what they say. They are congruent.

Long ago, Socrates said, "know thyself."

Long ago, Socrates said, "know thyself." That sounds easy. We live with ourselves, eat, sleep, think with ourselves—we know our every thought. Yet, sometimes we have to go to someone else because we cannot seem to understand who we are or what we are. When we cannot accept what is happening in our lives, we do not like ourselves very much. As long as we deny who or what we are, we will tend to confuse ourselves with our partners, our children, our colleagues, and, sometimes, even our material things.

Walt and Addie learned about others by knowing themselves first. Until Walt and Addie participated in a course in "Self-Understanding and Change Strategies" at a local university, they were not very different from Busby and Jolyn. In this class is where Walt and Addie first met. During the class they began their individual journeys into self knowledge and self discovery. This class was their first step in developing new patterns of communication—of listening, responding and sharing.

For example, prior to the course, Walt was in a dead-end job as well as in an unhappy marriage. His parents, brother, sister-in-law and some others in the community disapproved of Walt for getting a divorce—or so he thought. Their comments bothered him. Walt felt that many statements were made to let him know they were unhappy with him. He felt bad that he had disappointed his family. He tried hard to curry favor, to please, to gain recognition. In the process, someone suggested he might find help at the university. For this reason, he enrolled in the course in self-understanding. During that course, Walt began to understand for the first time the meaning of being an adult male; to comprehend what was meant by being totally separate from his parents, his brother and all other people. Walt began to realize that he did not have to be the heavy in the divorce and that he did not have to make his former wife the heavy. At this realization he began the conscious process of change. His first class assignment was to monitor his own behavior to find out what he did to try to make other people love him—things that he did that he really didn't want to do. He kept a written record of his behavior for two weeks.

What Walt learned about himself was interesting and enlightening. Three times in one week he had called his parents. Like a little boy checking in, he had called his parents to give a comprehensive report of his plans and an evaluation of his successes. He really had not wanted to call. He had done so because he thought they would "expect" his call. Also, when they said they would expect him for dinner on Sunday and would see him at church, he agreed to both. Again, because he did not want to disappoint them. Walt really wanted to go skiing on the weekend (something he had never done, but had always wanted to do,) but didn't dare tell them. Walt went to their home for dinner on Sunday.

At dinner on Sunday Walt found himself talking about things which did not interest him and even eating food he did not want or need. He ate to please mother. During his visit, his mother mentioned his former wife three times and each time Walt felt the need to respond and explain. He hated himself for this action.

This situation was just one aspect of Walt's behavior which he learned about as he kept a written record. Other things occurred about his behavior which were just as incongruent. This awareness of himself was his first step in becoming what he wanted to become. Once he was aware of how he behaved then he could know what he wanted to change.

Walt took on the self-improvement task of becoming more satisfied with himself—who he was and how he spent his time. Using the information he had gathered about his behavior, he was able to set up a program of change. Part of his plan concerned his parents. For example, he did not call three times a week. Instead he did such things as call (once in two weeks) and invite his parents to have dinner at a restaurant with him (something he had never done before). He made the appointment for more than two weeks away—and told them he would be away on the weekend and for them not to expect him for dinner on Sunday. (He did not **explain,** he simply informed). This was the first time he had not had dinner in his parents' home in a long time. Thus, he began a series of activities which broke his old habits. When he was successful, he rewarded himself—usually by mentally complimenting himself, but sometimes by doing something he really wanted to do, like skiing. And interestingly enough, Walt found that after those first few attempts to define himself the behavior was not painful at all. Also, he found his relationships with his family improved! Or at least he enjoyed being with them more. He was no longer concerned about winning their love and approval. He assumed he had their love and he was not especially concerned whether they approved, although to his surprise they did seem to approve most of the time.

A few weeks after that initial class Walt decided to change jobs. He admitted to himself that he was not happy as a service station manager. He had always wanted to sell—to go on the road—so he began the search for such a job. He found just what he wanted: insurance sales. Walt found almost no upper limit and he was good at the job. He began liking himself and knowing himself more each day. He developed a healthy self-concept, and with that positive feeling, he became freer in his willingness to share his successes and failures. Walt could communicate more openly because he was not afraid of who he was and what he thought and felt.

People are able to communicate more effectively when they feel accepted and safe. These acceptance and safety needs are enhanced through personal awareness and self acceptance. As Socrates taught us, you cannot know how to live effectively until you know yourself. Many other philosophers, teachers and religious leaders have espoused this same idea. For example, Jesus told his followers to "Love thy neighbor as thyself." Yet, with this laboratory for learning (i.e., self), available to each of us, we tend to be reluctant to delve into our own humanness, our own needs, our own desires and our own goals, to learn what we are like. Once we learn ourselves, we can then realize how much human beings have in common. All of us are more alike than different!

In our culture, we have focused on differences so much that we have neglected and almost forgotten the sameness in each of us.

In our culture, we have focused on differences so much that we have neglected and almost forgotten the sameness in each of us. We are enough alike to be able to predict how a person will behave under certain conditions.

This is the way experts on human behavior, such as psychologists and counselors, are able to predict behavior. Because the same behavior happens over and over again under similar conditions we can learn from the experiences of others. The fact is true that each individual is unique. But basically, the individual is uniquely important (not different) and is irreplaceable. I am arguing for a more open and flexible attitude toward life. That attitude is perhaps our best weapon against a world which is less predictable than we are. Also, with the extension of the individual's life into old age, more and more people live through several generations and through many external changes. Apparently personal flexibility is insurance against fear and failure in those later years when nothing seems very familiar or stable.

Flexibility is gained from a knowledge that we are all human and human beings are very much alike. We can know others if we know our-

We hide ineffectiveness with vagueness. "

selves. This is another of the many paradoxes of life. We lose our self-consciousness by becoming self-conscious long enough to know who we are and what we are. We cannot know human nature in the abstract. To the degree that we fail to understand ourselves we fail to understand others. To the degree that we fail to live effectively, we are ineffective in relating to others, as partners, parents or friends. If we cannot or will not accept our own humanness, how can we accept and appreciate the humanness of others? We hide ineffectiveness with vagueness, therefore, I am arguing for clarity. If one will state the problems of life clearly, alternatives can be found to solve them. Lack of clarity of problems and concerns can lead to deterioration and incapacity to cope with even the simpliest problems. Lena is a prime example of this type of confused thinking and inappropriate behavior.

Lena has just returned home to Larkin and the children. She has spent the last six weeks in a private mental hospital where she has undergone intensive chemotherapy. She could not cope with life before she underwent the treatment. Now she does not have to cope because no one expects her to. Now she can keep her world together through vagueness and confusion.

Lena
Larkin

The precipitating event that ended in Lena's breakdown was a simple daily activity. Larkin had called from the office. He had told Lena to be ready to go to the theater and dinner at 8 p.m. A couple had invited them to their home for drinks, the theater and dinner afterwards. Larkin had accepted. The outing was important to him politically so that they could be seen with these friends. When the couple arrived with Larkin to get Lena, they found her in an agitated state. Her problem: she could not decide which dress to wear. Her friend had to make the choice for her!

Larkin was equally agitated. But his agitation was directed at Lena. His anger had a target. Larkin's problem was clear to him. Lena, on the other hand, did not have any clear-cut reason to be agitated. To be concerned about a choice between two equally appropriate dresses was beyond Larkin's comprehension. He complained loudly. Larkin pointed out that he had worked hard all day, only to come home to this situation. "I deserve more," he told her. "The children obviously deserve more," he complained. His friends appeared to by sympathetic to Larkin. Or so Lena thought.

The next morning found Lena still awake. She had not slept all night. Larkin found her in the corner of the room talking to her imaginary mother. She sounded like a pleading child. She thought she was five years old and was with her mother. Her mother was helping her dress for a party. She was loved. She knew how to please mother and get her love. She could never quite please Larkin. He was alot like her daddy and she was a little afraid of him—of them both. Both husband and father were hard to please. Her mother loved her. So she would simply be a little girl again and everything would be all right. She could survive as Mother's little girl. She could not survive as Larkin's wife. She could not cope with the complex world as it was, so she made the world over as she wanted her world to be.

Lena found a way to cope. We recognize her way as self defeating and destructive. But the solution was effective for her. Her behavior was the only alternative she saw at the time. She did not (could not) discuss her problems with Larkin. She had never learned to state her problem clearly; therefore, she could not explore alternatives. She could control her world by making it over in her mind, and by so doing she could control those other people who expected too much of her.

Larkin was too busy solving his economic and political problems to spend much time being concerned about the mundane problems of wife and home and children. So long as the problems at home did not hamper his goals he had no major complaint. He did not see himself as especially demanding. Larkin felt that anyone who worked as hard as he worked deserved a peaceful home. He did not feel he expected too much from his wife at all. He only asked that she be presentable and look after the home. Larkin did not even question the money she spent. He felt cheated and angry that she should do this thing to him. He saw her mental breakdown as a real handicap to achievement of his career goals. He began a search for some way to solve his problem. He looked for some place to put Lena (to be looked after). He hired a maid to help with the home and children. Larkin stayed away from the house as much as possible. He assumed he would get things worked out sooner or later. But for the time being, he was really angry at his fate. The point never occurred to Larkin to find out what he might do to change the relationship or to assist in her (and their) rehabilitation. As far as Larkin was concerned, Lena was the only one with a problem.

How differently Bettye copes with her environment. Bettye has three children. Her husband, Euell, an army colonel, leaves her and the children for extended periods. Bettye always has been left with the major family decisions. She is the one who is responsible ***Bettye*** for what happens to the family. Bettye is the one who ***Euell*** helped the two boys plan their careers, obtain drivers' licenses, dress for their first dates and so forth. Bettye took her daughter to the hospital for her tonsillectomy and helped her plan her high school curriculum. Bettye is realistic and self sufficient. When Euell comes home on furlough or to move his family with him for a tour of duty, Euell has to fit into the family. He is the Colonel (i.e., leader) with his men, but with his family he is another part which is not very important to its daily interactions or to the system for getting things done. The irony is that Bettye sees herself as keeping the marriage and family together, but her capable and determined approach leaves little room for Euell. Their marriage is great when they were apart, but strained when they are together.

45

Bettye and Lena are similar in that they both are trying to make sense out of their worlds, and basically they both have done so independently of their husbands. Both husbands make good livings and both want their wives to be "good" mothers and proper wives. As far as personal satisfaction is concerned, both couples are pretty unhappy. Both marriages are weak and are held together by conventions or obligations. The couples have failed to plan and grow together. They married and expected their marriage commitment to be all inclusive in terms of their long-range goals. Neither couple anticipated the changing world of the developing human beings who comprise the marriages. Lena made her world over so she could manage it and Bettye made her world function without her partner. Both couples have missed the richness of sharing, feeling, being and becoming together and separately. The partners in these two marriages could be replaced, or removed, and the relationships would not be appreciably different. The marriages are stagnant.

A second marriage is a second chance to establish the kind of marriage one really wants. With maturity should come lack of self-consciousness and, thus, an appreciation of our need for each other and the joy of being and becoming. Growth is not limited to the period called youth. We are always in the process of change—and each individual can decide if the change will be in the growth direction or in the deterioration direction. A second marriage is a second chance to resolve to "know thyself" (and thus know others) and to "love thyself" (and thus love others).

With the continuing educational opportunities in almost all communities, a couple can usually find assistance in developing problem-solving and/or goal-setting skills. Even if no formal classes are available, a community school probably is available and these schools offer classes on demand. If a group of people requests a particular course, the class usually will be offered. Also, community members may want to develop their own study or self-help groups.

Individuals and couples can use various methods, many free or inexpensive, to continue their own growth. Every community has free cultural events. If one is near a major college or university, many cultural activities are available which are provided for the public.

Neighbors, friends and one's own family can set up their own "cultural exchange." For example, a family may try a new food, dish or different dining-at-home setting every few weeks. Neighbors or family members can teach each other new skills. Usually women exchange recipes, but males or females seldom exchange skills and information. This same principle could be practiced and could enrich everyone. For example, in one community, one woman taught several people to type, another led a study group on Child Development, another taught quilting and still another taught photography. This small group of neighbors enjoyed the contact with each other as they continued to expand their appreciation for each other, to develop new competencies and to learn new skills. One elementary school teacher in that community completed her master's degree after she retired from teaching, and another was learning to square dance the year she died at age eighty-six. Contrary to popular belief, people who are physically healthy can continue personal growth throughout life. We seem to get so concerned about appropriate behavior that we, as adults, are often reluctant to step out and learn new things. A tendency seems apparent in the older years to regress, to go back through those self-conscious years of youth. We tend to forget that the way to find security and enjoyment is through involvement. As we approach maturity, and even old age, to keep opening our minds to new experiences is especially important. If a couple will encourage each other and will support each other, new goals will continue to be exciting. Two people working together can produce far more than two people can produce individually. Synergism results when two people work toward the same goals and help each other feel safe and secure. The acceptance of a broad role for males and females, or the lack of concern for sex-role appropriateness, also enhances opportunities for self-development and personal growth. All new experiences enhance personal growth. Expansion involves risk. Risk means involvement in living. When growth stops, deterioration starts. The challenge then is to find ways to continue to grow together, to make the second marriage twice as satisfying as the first marriage was—even at its best. The potential for synergism exists if the couple will set new goals and personal development as their mutual goal.

ACTIVITIES FOR
INDIVIDUALS AND FAMILIES

To Be Completed Following Reading of Chapter 2

Topic A—FAMILY OR SMALL GROUP PROBLEM-SOLVING

Activity 2.1 Review the steps in the VISUAL method of problem solving (see Chart For Activity 2.1). Discuss the steps.

Chart For Activity 2.1

Step	Activities for VISUAL Method of Problem-Solving
1	Verbalize: Discuss problems and state clearly.
2	Identify alternatives: Prepare exhaustive list of ideas.
3	Survey advantages and disadvantages for each alternative.
4	Underline those advantages and disadvantages which are of major importance to persons involved.
5	Accept one alternative—choose the "best" one.
6	List what, how, and when to accomplish the accepted alternative.

Activity 2.2. Study the example of problem solving using the VISUAL method which is provided in the example that follows. Discuss the application of the VISUAL activity.

Example of Application of VISUAL Method of Problem-Solving

Step 1: **V** erbalize—Discuss problem and state clearly.
Shall we buy a new car?

Step 2: **I** dentify alternatives—Prepare exhaustive list of ideas.
a) Buy a new car (initial idea).
b) Keep old car (essentially "flip" side of option).
c) Lease new car (new idea-suggested by member of group).
d) Use some other means of transportation (suggested by budget counselor).

Step 3: **S** urvey advantages and disadvantages for each alternative.

Step 4: **U** nderline those advantages and disadvantages which are of major importance to persons involved.

Advantages

New Car—*Family wants one.* Status. Probably trouble free. Have for vacation trip.

Old Car— *Paid for. Low cost. Run ok-no problems. Low insurance.* Dependable. Good parts/service.

Lease— *Cost about like new car.* Trouble-free driving. Keep "new" car. Not "stuck" with car.

Public Transportation—Good bus service. *Cheaper.* Children learn responsibility.

Disadvantages

New Car—*Costs lots. Insurance goes up.* Might be "lemon."

Old Car— Lots of Mileage. Low status.

Lease— No equity. Loss of pride of ownership.

Public Transportation—*Inconvenient.* Low status.

Step 5: **A** ccept one alternative—choose the "best" one.
To keep old car (and gather more information about new cars).

Step 6: **L** ist what, how, and when to accomplish the accepted alternative.

49

1. What: Keep old car.
   How: Renew insurance.
   When: Monday morning.
2. What: Explore transportation needs of family.
   How: Topic for Family Council.
   When: Tuesday night.
3. What: Initiate search for information about new cars.
   How: Each family member makes choice and collects data.
   When: Report back one month from Tuesday.

Activity 2.3. Using the VISUAL method presented in Activities 2.1 and 2.2, solve some family or individual problem. Begin with a simple problem rather than a complex one. Use a chalkboard or a large piece of paper to record problem-solving activity similar in format to example provided for Activity 2.2

Topic B—FAMILY MANAGEMENT AND PERSONAL DEVELOPMENT

Activity 2.4. Develop a family housekeeping task/chore list. Involve the family in listing routine *tasks,* deciding *who* shall be responsible for each task, and *why* he/she is responsible. Discussion of time requirements and plans for rotating responsibilities also should be included. Review the example that follows and then complete your family list in the space provided.

Family Management Plan

Housekeeping Tasks/Chores: What they are, who will do them, and why this person is responsible.

Examples

a. Task: Weekly grocery shopping

_____

Who: Husband and wife

Why: <u>Time together. Both responsible for amount spent on</u>

<u>groceries. Keeps both current on problems of inflation.</u>

b. Task: <u>Empty trash and place for pick-up.</u>

Who: <u>Jim, age 8</u>

Why: <u>Shares routine task; has skill and necessary strength.</u>

Your List

1. Task _____

2. Who _____

_____

_____

_____

_____

_____

_____

_____

_____

_____

3. Why _____

_____

_____

_____

_____

_____

_____

_____

_____

_____

Activity 2.5. Agree on the basic *rules* for the family. An example of a basic rule is, "Anyone who plans to miss an evening meal will inform the cook of the intended absence at least one day before the occurrance." Discuss and record *why* they are important, and the *penalty* and *rewards* agreed upon for each rule. Review the example that follows and then complete in the space provided a list of basic rules with accompanying why, penalty, and reward for each.

Basic Rules

Basic Rules: What they are, why they are needed, what happens if they are broken.

Example

Give mother one day's notice when missing evening meal.	Expensive to plan and prepare uneaten meal. Family disappointed when members are absent unexpectedly. Shows respect for person cooking for family.	Disappointment of family. After two occurrences loss of use of car for one week.	Meals can be served on time—no waiting. Allows careful planning and scheduling. Saves time and money. Shows responsible behavior.

Rule	Why	Penalty	Reward
1.			
2.			
3.			
4.			
5.			

Activity 2.6. Explore personal development goals of each member within the family. As **members,** identify individual **goals,** record these in the space provided. Also determine what **resources** are needed, **who** else in the family will contribute and **how**. Establish regular time intervals to reassess goals and obtain "progress reports" in family discussions. Allow freedom to modify to change goals. Record the modifications or reaffirm the previously stated goal(s).

Personal Development

Goals: What are the personal development goals of each family member, what does he/she need to accomplish this goal, and how can, and will, other family member(s) help.

Name	Goal	Resources Needed	Who Will Help & How
Example: 1. Mother	Take walks	Time	Father will accompany
1. Mother			
2. Father			
3. Child A			
4. Child B			
5. Child C			

CHAPTER 3

LOVE: SYNERGY OR PIGGYBACK

An Old Man lived alone in the woods. A hundred acres separated him from his nearest neighbor. A Young Man representing the highway department approached the Old Man about bringing a road across his farm. The road would enhance his property, he was told. The road would also make the old man's home more accessible **Old** to his fellow man and would give him easy access to the **Man** city and all of its services. A highway could increase the value of his farm. These seemed to be sensible and de- **Young** sirable reasons for selling the land for the highway, and **Man** The Young Man assumed the Old Man would be de- lighted. The Young Man was prepared to make The Old Man an offer.

The Old Man listened politely to the Young Man as he offered the arguments for selling the few acres needed for the highway. But when the Old Man rebutted with his own arguments the Young Man was stunned. The Old Man conceded that what the Young Man said was true, but he saw those very arguments as reasons **not** to sell; he saw the advantages as disadvantages. The arguments represented intrusions into his privacy. The Old Man had built his home in the middle of his farm so he could have "room to breathe" he told the Young Man. He did not plan to sell, so the fact was of little concern what his farm was worth, and he neither desired nor needed access to his neighbors or they to him.

55

The Young Man could not accept the Old Man's arguments. He thought the Old Man was senile and ignorant. He could not see how anyone in his right mind possibly could prefer isolation to all of the services he could enjoy in the city—his friends, pizza in five minutes, the movies! He had no tolerance for the Old Man's position. The Young Man left in a huff, acting as though their difference in opinion was a personal affront to him.

The Young Man believes his position is **right** and a different one is **wrong.** The truth of the matter is the Old Man and the Young Man have different perceptions of their life-space needs. The Old Man needs lots of space, the Young Man needs little space.

Life space is both psychological and physical in nature. The Old Man needs a large physical space and he also keeps his psychological distance. He does not want to drain his psychological energy dealing with differences.

A couple has a life space that they share. The couple's life space is both physical and psychological. If the perceptions of the space needed and its use are similar, the couple will experience comfort. In this **comfortable space**, a couple tends to support each other's prejudices, notions, logical and illogical beliefs and so forth. To the extent that the support limits expansion of opinions, this support is harmful, or at least not growth producing. To the degree that a couple uses the comfortable space to develop common goals, establish priorities and support exploration into the edges of the **comfort zone**, mutual support is enhancing and helpful.

The Old Man, mentioned previously, married when he was quite young, took his child bride to his farm and built their home. They lived happily together until she died. He was the head of his household and his wife listened to him and obeyed his benign commands. They shared little information with each other and less with others. As long as they were together and as long as the world did not force its values upon them they could cope effectively. Their **comfort zone** was not often challenged from within or without. They have changed little. They will leave the world with basically the same values they held at eighteen years of age. They made a "good" marriage in that their marriage met their individual needs for intimate human contact while still maintaining privacy.

How do individuals pick out that person with whom they can share their life space successfully? The usual answer unfortunately is accidently, except perhaps with the hindsight of one marriage and the maturity of a second marriage. A mature couple will approach their relationship with some degree of attention to their individual and joint goals. But mostly we "fall" in love, and we have a tendency to believe that because we have had an expressively powerful experience (i.e., love feelings), it is good, healthy and true. We base our choices on our weaknesses as often as not. Ironically, love is defined as caring and showing affection, and also by another definition, weakness, as in love for drink!

When we think of the word love in the romantic sense, we think of a feeling—special feeling we have for another person. The word love represents a feeling of oneness in the closeness of sexual relations; a feeling that both partners succeed when one accomplishes a goal, and both share a disappointment when one fails. That is love in the usual romantic sense. Love is a valuable ingredient in marriage and probably a necessary ingredient for a truly successful one. When we experience these feelings we probably say we are "in love." We do not want to detract from that type of "in love" feeling. But love, in the sense that it serves one's own needs, is a relationship. So instead of being "in love" consider love feelings as "in a relationship." What does one get from the relationship; what does one give in the relationship? Does each person enhance the life of the other partner, or does love simply serve to support self-defeating or neurotic behavior? These are important questions to ask, and they imply important areas of potential problems. I will attempt to show the healthy "in love" relationships and the unhealthy relationships through the lives of several couples which are examined on the next few pages.

Jane S. is an attractive and successful college professor. She is basically a private person and admits enjoying competing in a "man's world." She is seen by her colleagues as a competent, demanding and somewhat unusual person.   **Jane S.**

Jane has professional recognitions, financial independence and job security. She describes herself as "needing to be alone" and "very proud of being independent." She is happy to be out of her first marriage which she describes as totally unsatisfactory. She says that she had little respect for her husband because he could not or would not make even small decisions concerning their home or family. He left the responsibility of the family to her. She was a strong, demanding, but supportive mother. Her children, though married and no longer living close, still rely on her for advice and occasional financial assistance. She thinks that to be "protected" and have her "burdens shared" would be nice. She is interested in establishing a long-range relationship and eventually a marriage with a supportive individual.

Jane describes her own behavior as independent (self-sufficient) and private (needing to be alone). She likes herself this way, and is consistent enough in her behavior that her friends and family expect her to behave in that fashion. When she acts differently, for example dependent and open, someone will remark, "Jane is not herself today."

With what kind of person did Jane "fall in love"? Jane fell in love with Jim, who is talkative, frank and open. Jim makes quick and easy work-related decisions, but is ultra dependent upon Jane's love and support, and he needs her attention *Jane S.* to give him a feeling of worth and accomplishment. Jim *Jim* does not make personal decisions without involving Jane, his mother and just about anyone he considers interested or concerned. He does not understand why Jane makes decisions without discussion. He feels she is overworking when she spends long periods in thought and study, and he worries that she is pushing herself too much. He protects Jane by planning activities which involve others and/or take her away from her work. Jim describes himself as open and sociable.

Conceptually, we can examine Jane's and Jim's relationship as two equal boxes which balance each others as illustrated in Figure 3.1. They complete each other's life. Each one is able to do those things the other is unable to accept as personally appropriate.

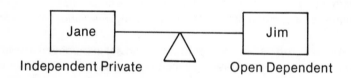

Figure 3.1. Opposites Attract When Individuals Limit Their Own Behaviors.

Will the relationship last and prove satisfying? The relationship can and will probably last if neither changes. The partners probably will annoy each other with the very behavior which makes their own lives complete, but the relationship will be generally satisfying. Jane will become annoyed with Jim because he is always telling things which she feels are of no concern to other people. She will wish she could have more time to herself, to study, think and prepare for her work. She will enjoy their togetherness, but at the same time resent his constant attention. She will long for a chance to compete with her colleagues and win through superior competence. Jim, on the other hand, probably will feel he is saving Jane from the hard harsh competitive world and will not understand her inability to enjoy this protection. He will be annoyed that she makes decisions without discussing them with him. He will be hurt when she does not include him in her activities.

What will happen if one changes and the other does not? Let us suppose that Jane begins to recognize her own need for control, independence and dominance, and she changes so as to accept these as appropriate ways to behave. If she is willing to be open and dependent at times, and if she expresses her feelings openly and honestly, she will not need Jim so much. Jim would lose his feelings of needing to protect Jane if she did not invite his protection. The balance would be disturbed because Jim's needs would not be met. Unless he recognized and changed his need to have Jane's behavior compliment his own, he would not find the relationship satisfying any longer.

A healthy relationship is one in which both partners are free to express a wide range of behaviors and accept the same from the other. For example, Jane could feel independent at times and feel that to be that way is all right, and she would express freely her independence. But at other times, Jane could feel dependent and feel that this behavior is all right, too, and she could freely express her independence. If she could accept these extremes for herself she would not need an opposite individual to complete her behavior needs. She would not expect Jim to behave in a consistent pattern, but she could accept him as behaving appropriately and consistently with his own needs—whatever that behavior might be.

In a healthy relationship being "in love" is choosing to be committed to a relationship with an individual whose life and values are fairly consistent and compatible with one's own. The **comfort zone** is similar enough to offer support and different enough to encourage growth. In this growth-enhancing relationship both individuals can evaluate their own behavior in terms of the goals to be accomplished. The goals of the two people in the relationship must be compatible for the relationship to be satisfying and long lasting.

Jerry and Karen illustrate what usually happens when a relationship changes over time. Jerry and Karen are a couple that "fell out" of love. More accurately, their relationship became dissatisfying and intolerable.

Jerry is a successful businessman. Highly ambitious, Jerry expects to be more successful than his competitors. Making money is his primary goal in life, and he believes this is the basic goal of all *Jerry* people. For example, he assumes that one goes to graduate school because it will enhance one's earning power, or that one buys a piece of art because it is a good buy, a bargain. He solves many of his problems with the use of money. Problems he cannot solve in this fashion are either ignored or attributed to some person or source external to himself.

Jerry is generous with his family. He supports two children, an aged mother and a chronically ill wife. He expects to be relieved of the burdens of the wife someday—by either death or divorce, but the latter is satisfactory to him only if one of his sons will assume responsibility for her. He describes himself as generous, good looking, aggressive and successful. These characteristics are to him synonymous with masculinity. He also says he is religious. To Jerry, a woman with feminine characteristics is helpful, subservient, grateful and religious. To him, the wife's responsibility is to attend church "for the family."

Jerry met and "fell in love" with Karen who was working as a secretary. She is ten years younger than Jerry, is attractive, conforming, and is from a large family with a limited income. When they first met, Karen was basically naive about the world. She "fell in love" with him and began seeing him more and more frequently. At first they skirted the issue of a permanent relationship or marriage. Nevertheless, eventually they began to dream of a life together and talk in general terms of "when we are married," or "when Jerry is free." (Neither talked about how this would be accomplished.) Of course, Karen did not push the issue since she believed that Jerry's responsibility was to take the initiative and also that to be assertive was not feminine.

Karen was a superb secretary and she soon came to the attention of supervisory personnel. Through encouragement and assistance from the

60

company she enrolled in several college courses (a good student) and eventually decided she wanted to attend college full time. She also decided to major in drama and hoped to become a writer or critic.

Jerry could not understand anyone's wanting to major in drama (what could you do with that in Middlesburg?). Even going to college seemed wasteful to him, especially for a girl. All the men for whom she had worked as secretary agreed she was a "real prize," and Jerry was sure they would continue to promote and help her.

After Karen became involved in courses and experiences in drama, her major field, she began talking excitedly about ideas she had encountered. ("Had Jerry read J.B.?" "Would he like to help with Town and Gown?" She attended local cultural affairs and began going to New York and London to see plays. These trips were made without Jerry. Jerry did not go with her and he offered the same arguments over and over: (a) he had no interest in plays, except comedy; (b) he needed to be home to see about his business; and, (c) besides, he didn't think Karen being seen with a married man was quite proper. She would be talked about and gossip might affect her standing in the community. Jerry was not concerned about being seen with her since everyone knew his wife was ill and men did that sort of thing anyway.

With her new experiences Karen's attitudes and beliefs changed. She learned to value honesty above approval, whereas before, the approval of others was more important to her than congruence. She became assertive; she refused to accept another's standards for her own behavior. She didn't discuss Jerry's behavior or marriage with him, but she planned her own life; she made her own commitments and she became involved in new experiences. Jerry tried to argue with her, to convince her that she did not want to change; he tried to bribe her to remain the same by offering her material things and even discussed his own plans for getting a divorce so they could marry. Jerry tried to force her to stay the same by bringing social pressure on her. He had his politically and socially powerful friends in influential positions to talk with her.

But Karen already had changed! She could no more *not* change—or go back as she had been—than she could force Jerry to change. No number of angry words—or kind words for that matter—could undo what was done. Their goals, values and desired life styles were no longer compatible. Karen didn't get tired of waiting for Jerry. Exactly the opposite. She was *not* waiting—she was growing and developing. In growth is always change. Therefore, if two people are to remain compatible and similar they must have similar experiences: cultural, religious, psychological and social.

Marriage partners may grow apart as surely as did Karen and Jerry in their relationship. Of course, Jerry still insists he is in love with Karen. But in reality, he is in love with Karen as she was when they first met—or more accurately—the idealized person he continues to identify as Karen. Seemingly, this growth/no growth process is one of the major problems of first marriages. Usually these marriages occur when the individuals are young and uncertain about their own goals and values. The experiences of the young mother and the young father are drastically different; for them to grow and develop apart is not unusual. The behavior is not intentional on either person's part. The partners do not understand their development, and therefore, they do not have the foresight to plan their activities so they can participate in similar growth experiences.

In a satisfactory marriage each needs freedom to develop independently.

While Karen initially felt stimulated by Jerry and the new experiences he offered, she now feels stiffled and constrained by him. Now that she has changed, Jerry does not "complete" her life. Therefore, their relationship will end. They will continue the process of drifting apart. In order to make a satisfactory marriage, Karen will need freedom to be herself and to continue to develop independently of the relationship. Since her perceptions of the role of the female have changed, she will expect to **get** as well as to **give** to the marriage relationship. Karen will need a partner who has a sense of independence and autonomy, one who will come together with her in the marriage to develop a relationship which is facilitative and emotionally supporting. The marriage of two autonomous individuals offers a promise of being synergistic and satisfying to both persons.

Unlike Karen and Jerry, some couples tend to drift toward each other. That is, they become more and more like one person. Actually, they become like the personality of the dominant partner. The weak one is something like a shadow to the strong one.

Evidence of this type of relationship is reflected in the relationship between Talmadge and his wife, Bea. That is the way Bea is seen: as Talmadge's wife. She introduces herself in this fashion and is introduced by Talmadge in the identical way.

Talmadge
Bea

Talmadge and Bea grew up in the same small southern rural community. As a young child Talmadge lived in a home with his parents and grandparents and in the community with several doting uncles and aunts. He had a special place among these adults because he was the first grandson. He was petted and pampered and waited on. For him to leave home for college was difficult but he did go and received a degree as a civil engineer.

During his college days Talmadge enjoyed the activities open to a youth away from the prying eyes of family and friends. To use his phrase, he "sowed his wild oats." During his college years, he experimented with sex and alcohol. But typical of men in his community, when he got ready to marry he "came home" and courted the girl next door. Again typical of that community, she was younger than he—by twelve years—and had not experienced the freedom of being away from the community. She had dated few boys and did so under close supervision of a suspicious father who knew "what it was like to be a man!" When Talmadge asked Bea to be his wife, he told her that he "respected" her, and he said that every man wanted a wife he could respect—one who was pure. He wanted a wife who had not experimented with sex, or even thought about it very much, and one whom he could introduce proudly to his friends.

Bea says that Talmadge taught her all she knows about sex, and she wonders if other couples their age have sexual relations as seldom as they. Bea wonders at times if they have a normal relationship, but she stops wondering and turns the question to an indictment of herself for her inability to be loving. She blames herself for not being able to "express her true feelings." She blames this upon the stringent child-rearing behavior of her parents. "They thought for a boy and girl to kiss was a sin," she says. Her family believed that "good girls" did not even think about such base things as sex, and even now as a middle-aged wife and mother of two, she still does not know if she is "normal" when she longs to express herself in a sexual way.

Bea worked for a short time. That was necessary so they could send their only boy to college. She really enjoyed her contact with the outside world until Talmadge complained about the strain her working put on *her!* He also told her that her working was difficult for him: he could not tolerate restaurant food and service at lunch was impossible. He felt he was developing an ulcer "from so much strain." So she quit work to stay home and "look after" him. (They lived happily ever after!)

If one invites Bea to dinner she will say, "I'll ask Talmadge and see if he can come." If you have dinner with them, you will eat whatever is good for Talmadge's (imaginary) ulcer. Bea gets up early to cook breakfast and get Talmadge off to work and then stays home to prepare his lunch and dinner. Seemingly her life is someway attached to Talmadge's schedule of survival activities (eating, sleeping, resting). Bea is too busy to read and too tired to sleep. She cannot understand how she can stay so busy and "not get anything done!" At this point in her life she seems resigned as she comments, "Well, I guess I am just slow and dumb! I work all day and don't accomplish anything!"

Neither Talmadge nor Bea has been married before. They have never considered divorce. As a matter of fact they seldom discuss any problem at all, so if they have any differences they have been left unstated. One is safe in assuming that neither will change in the years to come. But what would happen if one should die? Reasonably one could speculate that if Bea should die Talmadge would find a "replacement;" that is, another passive female who would provide service to him for room and board. This "replacement" would always be his "second" wife. Seemingly reasonable to speculate is that, if Talmadge were to die, Bea would be at a loss about what she would do with herself ("who would look after her"), and that she would move in with one of her children, her parents, or some other relative. She would never marry again because (a) to her would never occur the thought that Talmadge could be "replaced," and (b) she would feel that all of the things they owned rightfully belonged to the children, and, therefore, she would live as frugally as possible because to dip into the children's inheritance would not be right. Actually, if Talmadge should die, Bea would probably go into a state of shock and/or depression and become physically incapacitated for a period of time.

Bea has never developed a concept of herself that was not who and what Talmadge is and what he expects of her. She believes that women are defined as wives and mothers. Now that the children are married and have homes of their own she spends her spare time "helping the children out:" making clothes for them and the grandchildren, cooking their favorite dishes, and giving them food from her garden. Talmadge and Bea do not travel (because travel is too stressful for Talmadge) and hobbies (such as fishing, hunting and sports) are activities she believes are reserved for young (unmarried) girls and (married or unmarried) males. Their only activities outside the home are visiting neighbors, attending church and participating in a few civic clubs. Their entertainment circle is limited to their minister and a few relatives, and Bea "looks in on her parents" almost every day. Bea resents having to look after so many people, yet she feels this behavior is expected of her and the duty does give her a feeling of importance.

Bea is the prototypical "housewife." If she (i.e., the "stereotyped typical housewife") works (and she usually does sometime in her life), she does so for short periods of time "to supplement her husband's income" or to accomplish a specific and short-term goal. She does not want to work and her husband does not want her to work. We call hers a "piggyback" relationship: she goes piggyback through life being who her husband is. He carries as much life insurance as is possible so that his family will be looked after should he die. Since Stereotype Housewife has little sense of personal autonomy, she seldom initiates a divorce. If the husband seeks a divorce she argues that she has "given him the best years of her life." If she is divorced, she focuses on the event and not the process, and she fluctuates between feelings of self doubt, inadequacy and animosity toward her former spouse. She often honestly believes that her former husband is what he is today, because of her—"behind every great man is a woman"—and she does not understand how he could be so foolish as to fail to realize this truth.

The "Divorced Housewife" can never see herself as single, but only as without a husband.

The "Divorced Housewife" can never see herself as single, but only as **without** a husband. She does not have the option, socially, of moving in with family or children as the "Widowed Housewife" does. She needs someone "to look after her" as surely as Bea would should Talmadge predecease her, but for the Divorced Housewife, social mores are not so kind. If she does move in with a family member, the arrangement has to be temporary, so she feels compelled to do one of the following: marry again, become ill/disabled, or re-establish her identity and goals.

For Mrs. Divorced Housewife to "take her husband back" even after years of separation is not unusual. She dreams that he will become ill, or fall on hard times, and return, crawling and broken to her, to be taken back and nursed to good health, and, again, through her efforts, to build his respect in the community. If he has remarried she envisions his life as miserable and that everyday he suffers the pangs of regret. In her mind he is miserable in his new marriage, living with that "other woman"—for sex or money or some other quality which seems to her to be gross and ugly and destructive. She values this picture of him and keeps the vision fresh through frequent mental replay. Interestingly, if he should return, she issues an ultimatum which she has practiced mentally over and over again: that she will take him back **provided** thus and so. She threatens also that she will kick him out again should he fail to "toe the mark!"

Sometimes Stereotyped Housewife has an experience which brings about a drastic change in her personality. This drastic change may start a process which culminates in divorce and possibly a second marriage. (This kind of experience often precipitated by Mrs. Stereotype Housewife is returning to school, especially graduate school. She is usually from the privileged upper-middle class. The story of Agnes is offered to help the reader understand the dynamics of this precipitating event and the change process).

Agnes Scott was forty-two when she decided to go to graduate school to take a few courses. Her major motivation was not scholarly pursuit, rather she was afraid she was headed for a nervous breakdown if she did not do something. Her husband, Ted, **Agnes** a chemical engineer, made a good living and was a "good" **Scott** husband in that he provided well for his family, attended church and civic functions with them and helped and encouraged the children with their school work and career choices. The Scotts were members of a tennis club which provided wholesome recreation for the entire family, and all of the family was active in the Presbyterian Church. Most of their friends belonged to the same club and the same church.

Ted obtained his present job shortly after completing his Master's degree in chemical engineering. Over the years he has progressed steadily with the company to the position of section manager in charge of a research team. He and Agnes were **Ted** married when she was twenty-one, during her last quarter **Scott** in college. He was twenty-six, and a practicing engineer. They have three children, two boys and a girl. They live in a desirable section of the city, and the children have been successful in school, academically and socially. Throughout their marriage, Agnes has been encouraged by Ted to look after the family and do volunteer work in the community to satisfy her need to relate to others. He wants his boys to get a good education and his daughter to attend college until she meets "Mr. Right," or until she finishes a degree in education. He feels a daughter should be prepared to work "in case. . .," and that teaching is a good occupation for a girl to "fall back on."

For twenty-one years Agnes looked after her family. She did volunteer work. For years her major project was keeping the nursery on Sunday mornings. During their high school days Agnes went with the boys to their football games and with her daughter to dance classes. To use a biblical phrase, "her husband called her wonderful!"

Yet she was anxious. She had a gnawing feeling that something was wrong. Her last child would be leaving home next year, and her husband seems to need her less and less. He can now afford to buy the good life—she doesn't seem to be necessary to make life good. The children remain polite and attentive, but they no longer seem to need her.

Agnes had enjoyed her years in college. She had majored in sociology. At times she wondered if the situation had been right for her to have a good education and not "use it." She wondered if she could still learn. She wanted to know what life was like for the working wife. She began to feel that Ted demanded too much of her time for mundane things, such as entertaining his friends, supporting his organizations, preparing his meals. At the same time she felt he did not share enough of his time exchanging ideas and discussing issues. He seemed to seek out male companionship for that. Briefly stated, she felt as if she were being treated unfairly and that the world was passing her.

She wanted to know who she was and how she compared with others. Her husband thought she was being ridiculous and he was too concerned with his own career, sending his children to college, getting ahead, and so forth, to be concerned with his wife's problems (which he suspected were relatively unimportant and just a phase which would pass). His patent response to her searching questions about the meaning of her life was, "take some graduate courses—maybe art—and get out of the house more."

She did enroll in a graduate course, not art, but a course in counseling psychology. The catalog description appealed to her: the course was designed to develop **self-awareness** through communication exercises and **experiential group experiences.** She was searching for some answers for herself and this course seemed like a good place to start.

Ted was surprised when Agnes reported that she had enrolled in the course. He was annoyed when he learned the class would meet on Tuesday nights and, thus, conflict with their usual monthly meetings with their church school classes and Tuesday was their usual night to have dinner with his parents. However, he felt he could tolerate the inconveniences (for the semester), but he did suggest that she change courses to a more reasonable time period. But since this was the one she wanted, she remained in the class.

That very behavior, that is, registering for a course and refusing to change when Ted demonstrated his disapproval in his usual way, changed the rules of their relationship. Agnes had been controlled by Ted's suggestions and criticisms for so many years that she seemed like a new person to him. He resigned himself to making some adjustments to this new person. Interestingly enough, Ted had "an emergency" involving his research group and had to go to Washington, D.C., for an important meeting the very first night her class met. He invited Agnes to accompany him, and expressed disappointment when she told him that she could not go because she was going to class. For several weeks into the semester Ted kept "forgetting" the class and made appointments and commitments for himself and Agnes which had to be cancelled or changed.

She wanted to be someone who is as worthwhile apart from her family as any other human being.

Agnes was well-received by her classmates and she found empathetic understanding and support from her group sessions. In her group she began to realize that Ted was not responsible for her or how she felt, that she had control over her choices and that as a human being she had the right to make personally satisfying choices. She recognized that her own choice had been to define her meaning as the wife of her husband and the mother of her children; now she recognized that her needs were not their needs. They could not live her life for her, nor she for them. She was piggybacking and upon that realization she decided to change. She had no meaning except as wife and mother. While she felt she had performed those roles adequately, she decided she wanted recognition as **Agnes Scott**, a competent person "who. . .". She wanted to be someone who is as worthwhile apart from her family as any other human being. She wanted to define herself as a copartner (compeer) in a marriage, not as a Housewife for Ted, and not as a wife who took a few

68

courses to keep busy. She was bright and she believed she had the right to use her intelligence; she was energetic and she believed she had the right to be productive; she was curious, and she believed she had the right to be creative. She hurt and needed time to work through that hurt, and she believed she had the right to take that time. She wanted empathetic responses, not patent answers, to her concerns and she believed she had the right to assert that need and demand that her husband provide empathetic responses, or else she would seek them elsewhere.

Agnes did assert herself, and she did ask her husband for a different kind of relationship. Ted could not relate to this person whom he felt changed so drastically and abruptly. He confided that he did not know how to treat a wife as a "fellow." He could not, or would not, divert his energies from his work to learn other ways to relate. He felt he was successful as a husband and father. He blamed his problems on psychology and psychologists—and women's "lib." Eventually, they were divorced and both are happy again. Ted has married another housewife. Agnes is pursuing a career and is married a second time, not to a husband who looks after her (or she him), but to a partner who gives and demands equality in the relationship. This second marriage could serve as the prototype for a synergetic relationship—the antithesis of her first marriage.

American women are changing, and marriage and the family systems are reflecting that change. When one part changes, the other(s) must adapt or the system will disintegrate. We saw this disintegration in the situation of Karen and Jerry as well as with Ted and Agnes Scott. Jerry wanted Karen to remain as he perceived her, and not be in the process of **becoming.** Jerry's value system is **Karen** rather rigid and he views a wife as less capable, less **Jerry** assertive and less strong in a marriage. He cannot cope with the capable, competent, assertive Karen. In his mind he is "losing her." As she becomes more autonomous she will relate to others, males and females, as *compeers.*

We are finding more and more women moving in the direction of equality. They are getting support from each other. "Women's Lib has been a powerful influence and will not go away. Women's Lib is not a fad." More and more women are beginning to be assertive and autonomous, to want careers, to want to succeed and to have recognition. We are seeing more and more marriages of equals and fewer wives in the piggyback role.

> *A second marriage offers a second chance for two people to implement this attitude of equal importance and equal respect.*

I am optimistic about the changing role of women and the changing attitude about women in our society. A second marriage offers a second chance for two people to implement this attitude of equal importance and equal respect. A relationship of compeers is not only possible but encouraged. How much better this relationship is for the wife: she can share responsibilities. Such a relationship is also better for the husband: he is not totally responsible for the well being of the family! I believe such a marriage will accommodate change with enrichment. Compeers support each other in **being** and **becoming**. This type of relationship is synergistic. If a synergistic relationship was not developed the first time, perhaps it can be developed the second time around.

ACTIVITIES FOR INDIVIDUALS AND FAMILIES

To Be Completed Following Reading of Chapter 3

Topic A—ACKNOWLEDGING INDIVIDUAL BEHAVIOR THROUGH ROLE PLAYING

Activity 3.1. Assume you (couple or family) are confronted with the situation described below (Problem Situation 1). Using your usual method for solving problems together, come to a decision about the problem. Decide where you will go, for how long, and what you will do.

Situation 1: Planning a Vacation
The family has just been given $3,000.00 to spend on a family vacation. All of the money must be spent on this vacation. Decide what kind of a vacation the family will take, when and for how long the vacation will be and where.

What Were The Decisions
a. What kind of vacation?_____

b. Where will the family go? _____

c. How long a vacation? _____

d. When will the vacation be taken?_____

Activity 3.2. Relate the decision-making activity to individual behavior. One family member records the remarks.
a. How was the decision reached? _____

b. Who was the most influential in reaching this decision? _____

_____

c. Who talked most? _____

d. Who talked least? _____

e. Who supported whom?_____

f. How do each of you feel about the decision? _____

Activity 3.3. Role-play another situation (Problem Situation 2). This time exchange roles: husband play role of wife and wife play role of husband. (Each member in the group exchanges role with someone else.) As you role play this situation, try to act and think like the person whose role you are playing would think and act in that situation.

Situation 2: Moving to a New House
   The family has just moved to a new town. They are living in a hotel at company expenses at the moment but this arrangement will last only five more days. The family has to decide where to live. What will the family do? How much will the family spend for housing? What features are important? How much space will be needed?

What Were The Decisions?
a. Will the family buy or rent?_____

b. How much will be spent? _____

c. What features are important?_____

d. How much space will be needed? _____

Activity 3.4. Compare role playing to "typical" behavior in the family.

a. How was the decision reached in the role playing? _____

_____

Is this "typically" what happens in the family? _____

_____

b. In role, who was most influential in the decision?_____

_____

Does this person usually control the group? _____

_____

c. Who talked most in the role playing? _____

_____

Does this person usually have the most to say?_____

_____

d. Who talked least in the role playing? _____

_____

Does this person usually have the least to say?_____

_____

e. Who supported whom in the role playing? _____

_____

Is this "typically" what happens?_____

_____

f. How did each member feel in the role played?

Husband_____

Wife_____

Child_____

Child_____

g. What did each member learn about self?

Husband_____

Wife_____

Child _____

Child _____

h. What did each member learn about the person whose role he/she played?

Husband_____

Wife_____

Child _____

Child _____

Who was least influential in the group?_____

How did this least influential person feel in the "piggyback" role?

_____

Activity 3.5. Additional Exercises. Discuss among the family members what each learned about self and the dynamics in the family group. Role play additional situations (suggested by family members) until everyone has played every other person. Use the questions in Activity 3.4 to process the group dynamics and clarify the positions and attitudes assumed in the group.

Topic B—DEVELOPING AND USING SYNERGISIM IN FAMILY DECISION MAKING

Activity 3.6. Role play "Planning a Vacation" (Problem Situation 1) a second time. This time use the VISUAL method (see Chapter 2—Activities for Individuals and Families). Follow the steps as outlined. Use a large sheet of paper or chalkboard to display the information about the problem as it is presented. As the family works through the problem, members may find they need additional information. When this occurs, recess until the information can be acquired and brought back to the group. Don't rush the activity. Think of as many alternatives as possible. Write down the advantages and disadvantages of each alternative. Record every suggestion. Encourage creative ideas. After the family has completed Steps 1 through 6 of the VISUAL method, respond to the questions which follow:

What Were The Decisions?

a. What kind of a vacation?_____

b. Where will the family go? _____

c. How long a vacation? _____

d. When will the vacation be taken?_____

Activity 3.7. Discuss the dynamics in the family.

a. How was the decision reached? _____

b. Who was most influential in the group?_____

c. Who talked most? _____

d. Who talked least? _____

e. Who supported whom?_____

f. How did each member feel?

Husband_____

Wife_____

Child_____

Child_____

Activity 3.8. Additional Exercises

a. Compare the two methods (i.e., your usual method and the VISUAL method) of reaching a decision. Discuss the following

1) Which method involved most members of the group?

_____

2) Which method provided the most alternatives?

_____

3) Which method treated everyone with the most respect (equal)?

_____

b. Identify several real problems which the family can solve using the VISUAL method. Prioritize (rank according to importance) these problems, and make a plan for meeting as a group to work on them.

_____

Problems To Solve As A Family	Rank	Time	Day	Place
1._____	___	___	___	___
2._____	___	___	___	___
3._____	___	___	___	___
4._____	___	___	___	___
5._____	___	___	___	___

CHAPTER 4

BEING TOGETHER:
HELPMATES, PLAYMATES, OR CHECKMATE

PLAYMATES   CHECKMATES   HELPMATES

The Stovalls, Emmett and Ernestine, love to play chess. They enjoy matching wits and defeating each other. Emmett and Ernestine both pride themselves on their ability to out-maneuver and frustrate the other at this game. They say this is the only competitive game they play together. No doubt this is wise since they both accuse each other of going to any length to win: cheat, manipulate, distract! While they are obviously joking about the extremes to which they will go to win, equally obvious is that they both value winning. With delight the winner yells "checkmate" whenever the opponent can no longer maneuver.

Emmett
Ernestine
Stovall

To defeat another in a game of wits and skill is delightful, and a worthy opponent in such a game is appreciated. Some couples play the marriage game I call "checkmate" because they move or maneuver to counter and thwart each other. Such a game is fatal to a marriage. The game destroys both the "winner" and the "loser." Establishing a win-win relationship is the goal of a good marriage. I call a spouse in a win-win relationship a "Helpmate." This kind of marriage game (i.e., Helpmate) does not seem to be prevalent to our culture. This kind of marriage has to be learned, but few teachers for the Helpmate Model are available. Most people wind up being the kind of husband or wife they saw modeled in their own families. For many males the role they saw modeled was "checkmate;" for many females the role model was "playmate." The playmate learns how to piggyback, but never how to be a Helpmate. Few people know how to be effective partners.

Problems left unshared are unsolved.

If a "good" marriage means that a couple has developed an intimate sharing Helpmate relationship, then most marriages could not be called good marriages. This fact is true of first and second marriages. The problems in first and second marriages are almost opposite. That is, the list of problems of the second marriage looks like the list of the first marriage turned upside down. With first marriages most of the problems relate to immaturity of one or both partners, lack of understanding and preparation for marriage responsibilities and sexual difficulties. Children and money come in last as problems expressed for the first marriage, but these two are the major problems for the remarried. While partners in a second marriage have maturity and even insight concerning the basis of their problems, they lack the facility to share their worries and discuss their concerns with each other. Problems left unshared are unsolved. Unsolved problems lead to strained relationships. Strained relationships are not conducive to a "good" marriage. In the first marriage the couple tends to discuss or confront their conflicts head-on, but they lack the maturity and problem-solving skills to deal with them. In a second marriage the tendency is to *avoid* dealing with areas of conflict and, therefore, these areas fail to be resolved.

As children we are taught to share things, toys, food, and so forth, but we are seldom taught to share feelings, wishes and hopes. The intimate relationship of marriage can be threatening to the person whose usual way of relating is with caution and care. Interestingly, sensitivity to potential problems in the second marriage makes couples avoid confronting the issues. To deny areas of conflict is easier than to resolve them. Apparently from previous marriage experiences, couples have learned things that did not work when trying to solve problems, but they did not learn things that did work. They try so desperately to prevent crises that they create problems through their lack of communication.

We see this behavior enacted through Connie and Wilson. Connie was planning to marry a second time and she suspected that the marriage would drastically affect her relationship **Connie** with her daughter, Margaret. She suspected this, but she **Wilson** really did not confront the issue. She pushed the concern from her mind. She did not discuss it. She acted as though she could add a husband and son to her family system and these new people would adapt to that system: *they* would change. She did not anticipate and plan a *new* family system that included a **Connie** mother, father, daughter and son, that is, the new family **Margaret** which would result from the marriage. Connie's husband **Wilson** had died in a plane crash six years earlier when their daughter, Margaret, was only five. She was "daddy's girl" and Connie felt sorry for her; more so than she did for herself. Connie felt a little girl needed a father to love and protect her. Connie took on the role of mother and father. She and Margaret were inseparable. They did everything together—vacationed, talked, played. Connie was thankful for Margaret. To have a daughter now that her husband was deceased was a consolation and she found she enjoyed supporting the two of them. Connie was proud that she could stand on her own feet and make an adequate living. She was optimistic about their future when she met Wilson.

Wilson was divorced. He missed having a home and family. Since he had been divorced he had spent most weekends with Paul, his son. Paul lived with his mother some thirty miles **Wilson** away, Wilson looked forward to a time when he could bring **Paul** Paul to his own home and be with him in a more realistic atmosphere. When he and Connie married, Wilson moved into Connie's home. He was excited about having a home—a place he could bring Paul—and he was equally delighted at having **Wilson** a daughter. He hoped they would all be friends and enjoy **Connie** being together.

Wilson's salary barely was adequate to meet his alimony and child support, travel and expenses incurred in visiting Paul, and the left-over bills (lawyers, doctors) from his first marriage. About all he could do was keep himself together and meet his immediate obligations. Connie had some insurance money but she did not want to dip into that money, especially to take care of Wilson's financial problems which she saw as precipitated by indulgence of his former wife and their child. Wilson's non-acceptance of this idea annoyed her. She felt he was not assertive enough and that he still indulged Paul when he came for visits. More aggravatingly, she believed Wilson was concerned about his former wife's financial plight. Connie suspected he gave her money on occasions when he thought Paul needed things. Connie decided to discuss the insurance money with Wilson would not be wise because he might want to use it. She had her money earmarked (in her mind) for Margaret's education.

Margaret liked her stepfather, but having turned to her mother for support for so long, she continued to look to her mother as the authority figure. Connie enjoyed the idea of being married but she also continued to interact with Margaret as she did prior to her marriage. She expects Wilson to be part of the family on the one hand, but on the other hand she does not want to change her role as Margaret's provider and companion. She gets angry when Wilson does not assert himself and when he is ineffective as Paul's father, but she does not know how to interact or respond to her stepson in any meaningful way. Margaret resents Paul when he spends extended periods at "her" home causing her to share her things and her mother's time and attention. Connie is aware of Margaret's resentment and this leaves her feeling confused and guilty. Since Connie and Wilson are concerned about creating a good home for their children and a good marriage for themselves they do not want to admit to any problems. Like so many couples in a Second Marriage, they remain silent on these issues.

Discussion needs to be open and free.

Wilson and Connie are both sensitive to their own feelings, but they do not know how to deal with them effectively. Partly because they feel guilty and think they "should not" feel as they do, and partly because they do not believe any way exists to reach an agreeable solution to their problems, they do what many second marriage partners do: they avoid talking about the problems. Because of a prevailing tendency for partners in a second marriage to avoid confronting areas of conflict, I believe that premarital counseling or education for the marriage is crucial. Guilt can be incapacitating, and hurt or anger can be devastating. Using energy to avoid conflict is wasteful and counterproductive. For couples to discuss problems, set common goals and establish priorities together are important. Discussion needs to be open and free, without the presence of taboo subjects. Both partners should admit to being human and recognize that a tendency for people to be defensive exists and that compromise is difficult but possible. A *good* marriage allows and encourages sharing and yet allows and encourages each person to be independent, free and autonomous.

Two people working together can accomplish more than two people can independently. This is known as synergism. The following paragraph is a simple theoretical example of the synergistic effect.

A couple plans to purchase a new home. Assume that ten percent down is required for purchasing a home. If one partner (husband) has $3,000, he could purchase a $30,000 home. If the wife has $2,000, she could purchase a $20,000 home. The floor space, quality, and so forth, of the best house that either one alone could buy would be a $30,000 home. If they pooled their resources, they could buy any price home they desired *up to* $50,000. Therefore, if a $32,000 home was the best purchase for them at that time, this would be possible. By pooling their financial resources they have expanded their options considerably. While this illustration is based upon material goods for the sake of simplicity, the same concept works for solving any problems.

The productivity of a synergistic relationship is well worth working to attain. Two people working together can solve problems that two people working alone could never solve. Connie and Wilson have not learned how to combine efforts to solve their day-to-day problems. They work independently and even to some extent at cross purposes. They never have explored alternatives together and neither understands the motivation and desires of the other. They do not appreciate each other's attitudes and skills because they have not taken the time to communicate. While their individual goals are similar, they do not know this as a couple: they both want to be good parents and effective marriage partners. Their approach causes problems.

For example, Wilson tries to remove the pressure from Connie (his intentions are good) by going by himself to get and return Paul on weekends. Connie does not like for Wilson to be away from her on the weekends (her motivation is good) and is unhappy to think he is still concerned about his former wife's problems which appropriately are not his any longer. Both are angry, frustrated and concerned, not about the realities of their lives, but about their assumptions concerning each other. They could resolve these differences if they would only talk about them.

Suppose they decide to talk about their concerns, to help each other, to pool resources. One alternative they might examine is described in the following paragraph.

Connie has some (i.e., x amount) insurance money saved for Margaret's education. She shares this information with Wilson, and she also tells him she knows he does not have any money at this time, but she still does not want to use the insurance money to meet his present responsibilities. She also confides that she gets upset when he spends time with his ex-wife and resents the several hours he is away from home on Fridays and Sundays, especially on Sundays, when he takes Paul back home after his weekend visit.

Wilson confides he feels guilty about having to use most of his money to meet bills from his previous marriage, for alimony and for child support. He also informs Connie and Margaret that he feels he needs to spend time with Paul and is aware that this creates pressure for them, but that time with Paul is important to himself and to Paul. He wants Paul to know his father and to know that his father loves him. He expresses disappointment that the family is like two families on the weekend, and he also reveals that sometimes he feels left out when Connie and Margaret are together. He also notes that he feels somewhat guilty and ashamed that he cannot assume all of the financial responsibilities for his new family.

Margaret expresses her resentment at having to share her mother's attention and her things with Paul. She does admit however that to have a brother and father is nice and that she sometimes would like for Paul to live with his father all of the time.

With their feelings and problems identified, the family can explore alternatives which might help alleviate the situation and accomplish what each wants and needs. Suppose they explored many alternatives and the following solution was developed:

They will use the money Connie has in savings certificates as collateral to purchase a camping van and equipment. The family can then make a miniholiday out of most of the weekends with Paul. They can pick him up on Friday and then go on to a recreation site. The family members, including Margaret and Paul, can take turns in planning and serving dinner, planning family entertainment, cleaning up, and so forth. The family will be together in a new setting: their weekend home will be a camp site. They will have to organize and develop the rules for themselves as a family. This will be quite different from bringing Paul into their family and just adding him into the existing pattern. Wilson will be able to be with and provide for Margaret and Connie on the weekends just as he does for Paul, and Connie will be with him when he picks up Paul at his home. Paul will be a part of the "weekend family." Once they begin to relate differently and to have good feelings about themselves, they will have a happier family.

The camper/van also will be available for their summer vacation and, on occasion, serve as a sleeping room for the children, especially when someone wants to have a friend in for a visit.

With this open environment and sharing attitude the family might also work out a more reasonable visiting plan for Paul. Wilson might also realize that Connie enjoys working and Connie might realize that together they can and do make a more than adequate living. The children would develop a friendship and begin to enjoy each other. They would all lose their fear of each other. Margaret would learn, for example, that Connie can love Paul and Wilson and at the same time love her no less. Paul would learn that he does not always have his father's undivided attention, but this does not diminish his own importance. Connie and Wilson may learn that the husband-wife relationship is only a set of relationships, and that they can be responsible only for their individual behaviors and responses, but by sharing and trusting, they can gain more than they give. Wilson may realize that simply because he is a man, he is not responsible for everyone's happiness and well being. He will realize that he is no less or no more a person because of his obligations, but he will have to examine more alternatives in order to find appropriate ways to accomplish his personal goals. In other words, the family can become more fully functioning and optimistic. Optimism comes with choices. The enjoyment of life is in the *process* of attaining goals, and not so much in having attained the goals. The goals are the external evaluation or the effectiveness of the process.

A good marriage is a mutually satisfying dependent relationship built on individual autonomy that requires independent effort. We can use a team of horses to illustrate this dependent-independent relationship. Two horses can work together beautifully if they are harnessed to a common load. As a team they can easily move a load greater than one can move, regardless of the amount of strain and effort. But the team output requires individual input. The beautiful thing about the team of horses is that both of them are autonomous and fully capable or surviving and performing without the other. Separately, they can do things which they cannot do as a team. The reverse is also true.

Some marriages are like that: two individuals functioning together. Separately, they are complete, healthy, developing and satisfied. Together, they are able to compliment each other, accomplish new and different tasks, enjoy the rewards of working and being together and appreciate their differences and uniquenesses. They can ask questions of each other and expect honest congruent answers. They are not afraid to show independent strength nor admit to independent weaknesses. They are Helpmates. They are in a win-win relationship and are free to enjoy life fully, individually and together.

Some marriages are similar to a freight train. One is strong or superior, like the engine that provides the power, and the other is the weak or incomplete individual, like the boxcar. The boxcar is incapacitated without the power of the engine and the direction of the tracks. The boxcar attaches to the engine to be complete and fully functioning. The marriage of this type is fragile and brittle. Too much depends upon the strong one. The system is closed. The developmental tasks of everyday living are perhaps enough to destroy the marriage. This type of marriage is based on the belief that only one way exists for doing anything, and that only one of the individuals is capable of determining that right way. They can "checkmate" or destroy each other. Each hampers the other. Ironically, both partners suffer frustration and loss in this situation from which neither seems able to get out.

Establishing a "good" marriage requires more than good intentions.

Establishing a "good" marriage requires more than good intentions. Desire is necessary, but a satisfying relationship also requires planning together, individual commitment and energy, realistic evaluation and re-evaluation and frequent redirection. An understanding of interpersonal and intrapersonal relations is needed.

Emmett and Ernestine Stovall are a couple who are well on their way to achieving a good marriage. They have been married six years. This the second marriage for each, and both brought **Emmett** teenage children to this marriage. Since their marriage, **Ernestine** the children, Jody, Tony and Beth, have all finished high school and Beth is nearing completion of college. Jody and Tony are enrolled in the state university where both are successful students. Most of the behavior in this family is helpful and enriching. Individual differences are recognized and uniquenesses are **Jody** encouraged. Each seems to know how to supply support **Tony** and encouragement with freedom. Their marriage is dis- **Beth** cussed in some detail so that the reader can gain insight into the structuring of a marriage relationship which might be called one of *compeers.*

The Stovalls are strivers. Emmett has worked his way through sales force ranks to become office manager of one of the largest real estate offices in the capital city. He has achieved this position through hard work, self discipline, long hours and competence. His first marriage, to a highly emotional woman, had ended in divorce after fifteen years. When he was divorced he was debt ridden. Seemingly the wants of his former wife could not be satisfied. Regardless of his income, the outgo was greater. Doctor bills also had piled up. He had not known if his wife was sick (mentally) or selfish. This caused him guilt, anguish and frustrations. Her emotional outbrusts were frequent and unpredictable, but they were always followed by feelings of remorse. Then she would overindulge the children. Jody and Tony were fearful of their mother but they felt sorry for her. They chose to live with their father after the divorce. The mother felt unfairly treated throughout the divorce process and basically cut off communication with the children. "If you do not want me, I do not want you," she told them. They felt bad about the situation, but they welcomed the consistently reasonable woman their father married shortly after his divorce, and they felt they were fortunate to share the home established by this new marriage.

Ernestine was young when she was married the first time, before she finished college. She completed her degree after Beth was born. Ernestine's and Beth's relationship was more like that of sisters than mother and daughter, probably because Ernestine saw little of her husband and shared practically no part of her life with him. Ernestine's former husband made an adequate living as a representative for a large textbook company, but she knew little about what he made or how the money was spent. Her husband was only twelve years older than she, but still they had a father-child type of relationship. Their relationship had started out with her being a Playmate—manipulating, demanding, piggy-backing. However, as she matured, she began to recognize the kind of person she was becoming and she did not like what she saw. In order to bring about some changes in her own behavior, she went to work. As the years went by she became more devoted to her work than to her husband. Her work-related concerns became a substitute for love relationship with her husband.

Ernestine became a prized employee. She worked with a local company involved in industrial lighting and home decorating. She became highly recognized for her expertise and was sought after by companies planning to build or remodel. In addition, she wrote major articles for monthly trade papers for which she received a substantial salary.

Ernestine did not have an empty life, just an *incomplete* one. Occasionally she would feel concerned that Beth did not have an appropriate male-female role model from her and her father. She was still married when she met Emmett, who had obtained her services as a lighting consultant for his company. They found they were mutually attracted and began seeing each other, occasionally at first, then more regularly. After a long period of internal turmoil and ambivalence, Ernestine finally filed for a divorce on the theoretically simple grounds of incompatibility. The divorce was not contested, and Beth was given the option of living with either of the parents. She chose to live with her mother during the high school year; nevertheless, it was with some reluctance that she acquired a brother and sister!

Emmett and Ernestine were in their late thirties when they first met. They wanted to be married because they wanted to be together as much as possible. Both were willing to accept the responsibilities of a marriage that involved stepchildren and both wanted to build a new and different family, uniquely their own. Emmett and Ernestine wanted a family in which security would reside in the knowledge that each person had a place of importance in the family—each child and each parent. Theirs is a team effort: working together for a common goal, but valuing autonomy as individuals and encouraging independent thought and achievement. They present a common front: they are "the parents," not "the mother" and "the father." Their roles are broadly defined. The division of labor is based mostly upon interest and skill and both stay current concerning tasks which are to be performed so that at any time either could handle the family's business. For example, if one of them is in the process of purchasing land, the other simply keeps informed of the process. This way they do not spend unnecessary energy in accomplishing tasks and at the same time both are involved enough to have individual input. Either could assume total responsibility should the need arise.

These agreements were made prior to the marriage (and with the assistance of a counselor, an objective third-party) and the family has been able to adhere to agreements and plans surprisingly well. Both Emmett and Ernestine are basically healthy individuals and they brought few unresolved personal problems to their marriage. They know that a marriage is not built on good intentions so they established ample discussion periods, for themselves as a couple and for the family.

Their family discussions are held nightly, immediately following the evening meal. They refer to this as the "family hour." Emmett, Ernestine and the children feel that this regularly-scheduled time did so much to develop cohesiveness in the family. During the family hour they learned what made each other happy and sad; they learned of the day's successes and failures; they learned how to assist and support each other; they practiced problem solving; and they knew what was happening with each other. Although the children were at home together only a short period of time, all of them value having had experience as a family. They highly recommend a family hour.

In addition to the more general agreements they made, Emmett and Ernestine also decided to pursue recreational activities which they could enjoy together. Bicycling, swimming, golfing and bowling are some of the things they enjoy. They also travel a great deal. They rotate the responsibility for planning vacations.

Emmett and Ernestine have not compartmentalized their lives nor their roles. They work as compeers. They are equal.

Emmett reports that he is happy with his second marriage. He hypothesizes that most first marriages are unsatisfying because as youth we tend to marry opposites, and that most second marriages are satisfactory because as mature adults we tend to be attracted to people who are similar. The youth has not yet defined himself and looks for completion in someone else. The mature individual has a definition and acceptance of self and looks for an individual to compliment that concept.

Ernestine concurs with his analysis, but she attaches a meaning to maturity to include a feeling of self worth and self esteem. She believes that mature individuals perceive the world as complex and enjoy dealing with complexities. Therefore, problems for mature individuals are seen as challenges and they find excitement in solving them.

Emmett and Ernestine certainly represent self-defined autonomous individuals. They have as many potential problems as any other couple with children from previous marriages, but they have successfully confronted those issues and they have treated life as a challenge. They have added immeasurably to their own growth through their willingness to learn from each other, and they have taught their children how to solve problems. Especially important is the fact that parents do this in our society. Our information overload creates an environment in which people foolishly seek simplistic answers. Culturally we encourage immaturity: immature expenditure of resources, immediate gratification, and personal irresponsibility. We let our advertisers tell us what we want and our entertainers tell us what we think. We need strong parents who work together to help children learn the skills of living so that they can be creative individuals, effective partners and loving parents.

ACTIVITIES FOR INDIVIDUALS OR FAMILIES

To Be Completed Following Reading of Chapter 4

Topic A—IDENTIFYING TYPE OF RELATIONSHIP REVEALED THROUGH VERBAL BEHAVIOR

Activity 4.1. Study characteristics of relationships provided in chart for Activity 4.1. Learn to differentiate among the three types of relationships.

Chart for Activity 4.1.

Type of Relationship	Characteristics
HELPMATE	—Message is clear and crisp. —No hidden meanings are present. —You said what you meant (thought and felt). —You are responsible for your own feelings and actions—do not make someone else responsible. —You are equal and autonomous but care what the other person feels and wants.
CHECKMATE	—Message has underlying meaning which is different in tone and content. —You put the person on the defensive. —You offer a double-bind choice (no win position). —You use power to control. —You are in a superior position.
PLAYMATE	—Message has double meaning. —You use flattery to gain control. —You appear dependent, helpless or inferior. —You ask the person to be responsible for you. —You imply an exchange of favors.

Activity 4.2. Examine the communication between John and Cathy (husband and wife) in the statements that follow. For each statement identify the type of relationship (i.e., helpmate, checkmate, playmate) and write the message revealed or implied in the speaker's statement.

Statement 1—Cathy to John:

"John, I want to see my parents—maybe spend a week with them. I would like for you to go also, but if you had rather we do something else when you have a week free, I can accept that. I'll try to work out as convenient a time to be away as possible."

Type of Relationship _____

Message _____

_____

_____

ANSWER

Answer to Statement 1—Type of Relationship   Helpmate

Message   I love you, and I love my parents. Both relationships are important to me. One relationship does not depend upon another—I am willing to make my wants known.

Statement 2—Cathy to John:

"John, you're going to a Conference in Chicago next month. I think it only fair that I do something I want to do. I'm going to spend a week with my parents."

Type of Relationship _____

Message _____

_____

_____

ANSWER

Statement 3—Cathy to John:

"Johnny, if you'll let me go see my parents for a week, I'll go fishing with you and camp out for a week—like you have been wanting me to do. What do you say? Even trade?"

Type of Relationship _____

Message _____

_____

_____

_____

_____

ANSWER

Statement 4—John to Cathy:

"Sweetheart, I know how much you want to go to see your parents next week, and I want to go, too. But the Parnes have asked us to join them for a fishing trip next week. It could mean an account for me. We need to put up a "solid front." You do want me to get the account don't you? If I can get Parnes' account, we can afford to take lots of time off."

Type of Relationship _____

Message _____

_____

_____

ANSWER

_____

Answer to Statement 4—Type of Relationship   Checkmate

Message   You can't desert me in this life-or-death matter—if you do, you are not a "good" wife, and I am such a "good," hardworking husband.

Statement 5—John to Cathy:

"Baby, if we can entertain the Davises this weekend—and if you'll be a good hostess—I'll buy you that pretty outfit you wanted. You sure would look pretty in it—and it would make me proud to show you off!"

Type of Relationship _____

Message _____

_____

_____

ANSWER

_____

Answer to Statement 5—Type of Relationship   Playmate

Message   I'm okay, and you are okay if you make me look good; you will have to earn my approval (love).

Statement 6—John to Cathy:

"Cathy, I know it's important to you to spend some time with your parents. I would enjoy being with you, but right now I prefer to devote my individual attention to several important accounts. When you get home, we'll spend the weekend together."

Type of Relationship _____

Message _____

_____

_____

ANSWER

Answer to Statement 6 Type of Relationship   Helpmate

Message   You're okay, and I'm okay. We don't have to prove we are important to each other. I do not want to control you, nor do I want you to control me.

Activity 4.3. Write statements *Typical* of what you might say. To do so, assume you are talking with a family member. Write a "typical" statement you might make for each of the following five topics:

Exercise 4.31. Something you would like the family members to do.

_____

_____

_____

Exercise 4.32. A foolish mistake you made.

_____

_____

_____

Exercise 4.33. A visit from the in-laws.

_____

_____

_____

Exercise 4.34. Attending worship service.

_____

_____

_____

Exercise 4.35. Use of leisure time.

_____

_____

_____

Activity 4.4. Examine your "typical" responses in Activity 4.3. Use Chart 4.2 to help in the analysis. Note in the margin opposite each exercise in Activity 3 the type of relationship your statement reveals.

Activity 4.5. Ask yourself whether or not you want to establish a helpmate relationship within your family. If so, rewrite in Activity 4.3 any statement which was not already a helpmate type of relationship. If more practice is needed, use additional paper to write other statements.

Activity 4.6. Now that you understand the characteristics of a helpmate relationship and if you want to improve your helpmate relationship, practice verbal communication using helpmate statements in your daily activities.

Activity 4.7. Introduce the concept of types of relationships to the entire family. In doing so, repeat Activities 4.1 through 4.6 with the family. As a family, discuss the dynamics of the family when this approach is used.

Topic B—IDENTIFYING AND ASSESSING FAMILY INTERACTIONS.

Activity 4.8. List major responsibilities assumed by husband, wife and both under the following categories: work, home, family and community.

WORK

Husband's Responsibility _____

_____

Wife's Responsibility _____

_____

Shared _____

_____

HOME

Husband's Responsibility _____

_____

Wife's Responsibility _____

_____

Shared _____

_____

FAMILY

Husband's Responsibility _____

_____

Wife's Responsibility _____

Shared _____

_____

COMMUNITY

Husband's Responsibility _____

_____

Wife's Responsibility _____

_____

Shared _____

_____

Activity 4.9. Analyze the responsibilities listed in Activities 4.8 and then answer the following questions:

a) Do the responsibilities in Activities 4.8 reflect close adherence to

stereotyped sex roles? _____

If they do, what are you communicating to each other and the

children by adhering to this standard? _____

_____

b) Re-examine the responsibilities listed in Activities 4.8. Are the re-

sponsibilities equitable? _____

c) Are the areas of responsibility based on interest and skill?

_____

d) Consider and list alternatives. Determine some things you can do together (such as clean yards), some things you can exchange (such as painting house and carpet cleaning) and some things you can rotate (such as meal preparation). _____

_____

_____

_____

e) Try out some of the alternatives. Following the try out, discuss together the new experiences. _____

_____

_____

_____

Activity 4.10. If children are involved, use a similar procedure to Activity 4.9 to help them expand their concept of appropriate behavior and open new options for skill building as well as family living.

CHAPTER 5

PARENTING AND
FAMILY LIFE-STYLE BUILDING

A family is a social system. Since the family is a social system, it is susceptible to human engineering. Some people are repelled at that thought and therefore try to deny its truth. But human beings establish and comprise the system, and thus the system can be manipulated or managed by them. Parents are especially influential on the family as a social system because children, as dependents, must go to and through them in order to meet their survival and psychological needs.

A second marriage resulting in a merged family offers parents a new opportunity to develop the kind of social system they desire.

A second marriage resulting in a merged family offers parents a new opportunity to develop the kind of social system they desire. Effective parenting behavior produces well-adjusted children who can get along in the world outside the home. In other words, a child's behavior can be understood as learned responses which are useful in meeting personal needs and goals.

How does a child get what he/she wants? Primarily through trial-and-error or random behavior, initially. The child is dependent on the parent, dependent on the parent, therefore, he/she acts in some manner to meet some egocentric need. This is random behavior which I shall call **activity behavior.** This term simply means that the child wants something, i.e., moves in some fashion. The parent reacts to the activity behavior and in so doing rewards the activity behavior. The child interprets the "reward" in his/her own way. If the child likes what happened after certain activity behavior he/she will then use that same activity behavior whenever he/she wants to accomplish that particular goal. The activity behavior becomes one's style for meeting personal needs. In this way the child learns "appropriate" behavior for a particular family system.

By examining two different parental responses to a common activity behavior we can see how a child develops a behavior repertoire or style of behaving.

A three-year-old wants to take a book from an older sister (Activity Behavior 1). The sister tells him/her, "No, I am using the book!" The three-year-old cries (Activity Behavior 2). No one responds to the Activity Behavior. The sister continues to read her book, and the mother continues what she is doing (Reward 1). After a short period of crying the three-year-old holds his/her breath and then tries bumping his/her head on the floor (Activity Behavior 3). Mother leaves the room (Reward 2) and the sister turns her back and continues to read (Reward 3). The three-year-old gives up, and lies on the floor and sobs quietly for a few minutes. Before long he/she is in a play area and happily playing with toys.

We can predict that the child interprets crying, breath holding and headbanging as nothing extra special and that this behavior is a good way to lose mother's attention and presence. We can also predict that this three-year-old will not persist in this activity behavior.

Let us replay this activity behavior with a different response and see what happens. A three-year-old wants to take a book from a sister (Activity Behavior 1). The sister tells the child. "No, I am using the book!" The three-year-old cries. Mother stops what she is doing. She explains that the sister is in school, that this is a school book and that the sister needs it. She also tells the child that he/she might tear it (Reward 1). The more she talks the louder the three-year-old yells. Mother offers the child a cookie as a peace offering (Reward 2). The child holds his/her breath and bangs his/her head. The mother gets excited. "You'll hurt your head," she tells the child (Reward 3). The child persists in the behavior and Mother panics because she is afraid he/she will die because the child is "turning blue." She grabs the child and runs and dashes water on the child's face (Reward 3). When the child catches his/her breath, Mother is so relieved. The child lays on her shoulder and sobs. She pats and cuddles the child and walks him/her to sleep (Reward 4). Later she talks to her husband and others about the child's "breath holding and turning blue." The child is aware that he/she has created a great deal of excitement.

We can predict that this three-year-old interprets breath holding as both powerful and super effective for controlling one's environment. The next time the child wants Mother's attention or wants to be held and coddled, he/she will know how to bring about such behavior. The child has learned what I refer to as *eccentric consequences.*

Eccentric consequences are logical and appropriate only in the unique social system, (such as the family), where they were learned. Consequences which are logical and predictable in the world outside the family social system I shall refer to as predictable consequences. The child who learns eccentric consequences in his/her home is at a disadvantage in the social systems outside the home, such as the classroom, because the child does not understand the predictable consequences of his/her behavior, and, therefore, the specific behavior will be at odds with the norm for his/her group.

I have argued that the family is a social system which is subject to human engineering. I have also indicated that each child develops appropriate behavior for his or her unique family. I have also implied that disruptive or negative behavior which is evidenced outside the home is to a great extent the result of a child experiencing eccentric consequences in the family system. I believe that parents who teach eccentric consequences are doing children a great disservice. These parents will bump against the real world and its logical or predictable consequences. The child who does not know how to manage his/her world to benefit from the predictable consequences is not in a competitive position. Such a person is set for disappointment and maybe even failure.

To the extent that both partners are psychologically healthy and aware of their own needs they will be open to new experiences and able to establish a healthy family system.

Developing the family social system to produce the desired results requires more than "doing what comes naturally." Setting up a family system where children will experience predictable consequences requires information, self-awareness, and parental agreement and commitment to that type of family life-style. Parents with unresolved problems or neurotic needs cannot develop a fully-functioning healthy system because their responses will be influenced by those specific problems or needs. For example, if the parents need evidence of love and approval from the children at every turn, their responses will be self-conscious and their goals short termed. Some people believe that behavior outcome planning and systematic reinforcement is cold and calculating and, therefore, antithetical to love and caring. I believe the opposite. I believe if we care enough we will help the child recognize and use the predictable consequences of society's social systems. I believe we have done the child an injustice when he/she believes the family's eccentric consequences represent the norm for society. I believe this confusion between eccentric and predictable consequences is the major reason children get in trouble. Children are attempting to make sense out of the cultural social systems and the consequences are incongruent with those consequences they learned at home.

Reese Lee, a probation officer, has a case load of individuals who had committed delinquent acts because they had been confused about the consequences of their specific behaviors. These persons confronted a social system which was at odds with what they accepted as appropriate behavior. One such delinquent person is Bobby.

Bobby, who is twelve years old, was assigned to Mr. Lee because he had stolen a bicycle. Mr. Lee was impressed with Bobby's sensitivity to others, especially younger children, and his   **Reese Lee** seeming anguish at having done something everyone   **Bobby** considered wrong or bad. He seemed truly contrite about the illegal act and welcomed Mr. Lee to his home to work with him and his family. His story, as uncovered by Mr. Lee, graphically illustrates the appropriateness of his behavior in his family.

Bobby's mom and dad both worked. Until very recently they had made a good living. Bobby enjoyed the things the family did together. He especially enjoyed having his mother and dad go with him to basketball games when he played. Everything was just fine until Bobby's father lost his job when the auto plant for which he worked closed. He had been employed there five years—as long as Bobby could remember.

ARGUMENT   DISAGREEMENT   TENSION

When parents argue and disagree, tension is produced in the children. The result often is an interruption in the family-life style.

After staying home a few weeks, his father began searching for new employment. Tensions mounted during this period of time and Bobby overheard what he thought were fights and arguments between his parents. Sometimes his mother cried; sometimes his father seemed angry.

Then his father landed a job with a construction company. This new job had its advantages and disadvantages. He could make a good salary, but his first assignment was to work on a bridge some two hundred miles away. Bobby was in school and his mother worked. They could not go to the work site to live, and his father could not commute daily. With work possible and money needed his father worked overtime and was away for several consecutive weekends. He did not come home even after Bobby phoned him and told him about the big game coming. Bobby's father did not come even after his mother talked with him and told him how difficult managing Bobby was without him. Bobby got the impression that his family was coming apart. His mother seemed irritable. He believed his father was too busy for him and that his mother was too preoccupied to care about him. Bobby had seen his family rally to help when a crisis existed: when granddad was sick; when Uncle Ted went to service; when dad lost his job; when Aunt Agnes dropped out of college; and so forth. Bobby thought he had found a solution. He would create a crisis. That behavior would bring dad home and make mother notice and care.

Bobby stole a bike. He created a crisis. The action worked. Mother called dad and he came home the next day and stayed for almost a week. Mother and dad talked in quiet voices for long periods. Everything seemed fine between them. They spent a great deal of time with Bobby. They talked to him. They discussed the pros and cons of dad's new job. Mom considered taking Bobby out of school and quiting her job and moving to the work site with dad. Everything else was forgotten in the crisis. Bobby validated his notion that he could control the family by creating a crisis. The family would rally around him when he had a problem. Over the years Bobby had interpreted the family behavior in such a way that he got the following impressions:

1. Arguments, disagreements and tension are dangerous and "should not" happen.
2. Involvement in the family is necessary for a member of the family to feel included.
3. Forces outside the family which they cannot control bring members closer together.

Based on eccentric consequences taught in the family, Bobby's behavior was appropriate and quite effective. The family has good intentions. If they work with Mr. Lee, they can probably bring their family to a new way of functioning where rewards will be consistent with the more predictable consequences of society.

Discussion, open and honest, with all of the family present would have helped this family immeasurably. Had Bobby known what was going on with his father he would not have believed that the tense discussions behind closed doors meant that someone was angry with someone else. He would not have thought that to leave home for a brief period to work would have destroyed the family. Had they discussed what was happening they might have solved the problems in some other

104

way. Bobby did what we all do. In the absence of data or information we create our own data. If we are sophisticated and knowledgeable (objective perhaps) when we make up data, we call the process hypothesizing or theorizing.

With a second marriage a family is often comprised of children of previous marriages and parents of previous family relationships. These people bring their eccentric-consequence expectations with them. The establishment of a satisfying family life-style from such a beginning is no accident. This establishment requires sustained attention, accurate information and cooperation. Helpmates who know who they are and are comfortable with themselves have the potential for achieving success in their parenting roles as they establish their second families.

Just about all of the potential satisfactions and potential hazards of a second marriage are tied up with the success or failure of the new family constellation. Because of the importance to the couple individually and because this success is separate from their other relationships they should expect tensions between themselves as they deal with family development problems. A couple's personal relationship is affected by their success or failure to merge a family with shared values and goals. Since each individual brings his/her own expectations to a new family, conflicts are sure to arise. Concerns relating to the family should be given priority attention by the couple, and prior to their marriage they should make a pact to share feelings in this area—even painful feelings.

A family is certainly not dependent on biological relatedness. For centuries human beings have been successfully rearing children of others. Adopted children are prime examples that this fact is so. A family is a social relationship, and a biological relationship need not exist for the social relationship to exist. Just as a parent's relationship with a child is not dependent upon the quality of the parent-parent relationship, the relationship among family members of a second marriage is not dependent on previous family relationships. Old patterns of relating can be broken; new patterns can be established. With a second marriage the partners have a new opportunity to establish the kind of social system they view as healthy and fully functioning. As I have indicated earlier, the family life-style may be consciously modeled and developed. To the extent that both partners are psychologically healthy and aware of their own needs they will be open to new experiences and able to establish a healthy family system. However, a new family system built on neurotic or pathological behavior will be as neurotic or pathological as the most unhealthy parent.

If we examine the interactions between Art and his parents, we can understand the impact the neurotic parent has on Art's perceptions. Art's parents are his natural parents, but ***Art*** similar interactions are evident in merged families also. However, had this incident been cited as a merged family situation, most likely many people would have assumed that the parents behaved as they did because they were into a second marriage.

Art is an only child. His father is a well-to-do dentist turned businessman, and his mother is a typical housewife. When Art was in high school his father bought him a Volkswagon as a bribe to improve his school work so he could get into a "good" school. When his grades and work attitudes did not improve, his father told him he would have to park the car until the grades were improved. Art was angry. He begged, cajoled and threatened. (At one point Art threatened to run away and join the Army!) A few days after delivering the ultimatum to Art, his father left home for a three-week business trip. Before the plane was hardly off the ground, his mother asked Art to run some errands for her. Art told her that he would do what she wanted if she would let him drive his own car until his father returned. She agreed. She told him that he could have his car while his father was away, but that he was not to let his father know. She said that she felt justified in this because her husband has left her "stranded" for three weeks and because he did not invite her to go with him on the trip.

Of course Art was pleased. He told his mother she was the greatest. He learned one way to get what he wanted. From these messages, Art gets the impression that: (1) Mom's the good guy—Dad's the bad guy; (2) fathers punish and we (mom and son) have to join forces to protect ourselves; and (3) "they" owe us a living and "we" deserve rewards. Art's mother could be called the "Great Manipulator." She is neurotic and through her example Art is developing habits and expectations consistent with his family's Eccentric Consequences and this puts him in conflict with society.

Art's parents do not communicate; they act first, then react! They do not set common goals since reaching agreement on techniques for shaping Art's behavior has never occurred to them.

Children need consistency because they need to know where the limits are. If both parents agree on the limits and support each other in setting those limits, the child will accept the limits (whether permissive or structured). But when children do not know where the limits are, they are constantly checking things. They wheedle, manipulate, whine and lobby to get what they want. Like the gambler, to quit is hard—whether ahead or losing—because they never know when the next pay off will occur.

That Art thinks the world owes him a living is no wonder. He assumes that if he's losing now (poor grades, no car privileges), his luck will change. And indeed it will—at least in those areas he can manipulate, or his parents can manipulate for him.

Part of the problems in the dynamics of this family is their acceptance of the idea that discipline is the sole responsibility of the father. The members of Art's family believe that only certain behavior is appropriate to individual family members. That Art is reluctant to grow up and assume the man's awesome responsibility of making the living, supervising the children, and appeasing the wife is not surprising. This is the kind of model he has in his father.

The dynamics are different in Vance's family. In his family both parents are equal and both can and do speak for the family. The decision of one parent is supported by the other   ***Vance*** parent.

Vance told his mother that he wanted to participate in the high school band and that this would mean going to many band practices after school and to performances on frequent occasions. He wanted to know if he would be permitted to join the band, and if so, if he could meet the obligations of membership. Vance's mother, Martha, suggested that this would be a good question to bring up in the family council.

Vance knew what this meant. This suggestion inferred that such participation in the band was an important decision to make because it was something which involved the whole family—his mother, stepfather, sister and stepsister. Because the situation was a family problem, it needed to be a family decision. They would arrive at their decision democratically. Their family council met every Tuesday night but any family member could call a special session at any time. Vance decided to wait until the regular Tuesday night council to present his problem. This gave him time to plan some alternatives to propose.

During the family council the group agreed that Vance would probably enjoy and benefit from the band experience. They also agreed that the family car could be used for transportation when needed, but

Vance should bear some of the expenses. The family, as a group, decided that Vance should pay for the gas and that these payments should be made weekly. In addition, Vance would pay that part of the insurance which would be added to the premium when he was added as driver. (He was just sixteen and had his first license.) He accepted these decisions as reasonable and valid.

Vance was a good student. He worked part-time, and like the other family members he received a modest allowance. (The amount of the allowance for all of the family members had been worked out in the family council also. The amount each person received was based on three factors: family resources, needs and ability to earn.) Vance was able to pay for the gas and the insurance without great strain, and he did so for some weeks without incident. Before long however he was confronted with a problem.

A rock group brought a concert to town. Vance's idol was a member of the group. Vance had to go! He bought tickets for himself and his girlfriend, and then he borrowed five dollars from his youngest sister so that they could go to dinner. Vance really enjoyed the date and the concert. The occasion was a special time to remember.

The next week, Vance drove the car as usual. He made no extra money and since he had used his allowance he told his dad that he wanted to put the gas "on the cuff," that he would pay it off later.

His Dad indicated that was not the agreement and simply reminded him that he was allowed a one-week deficit. Since he had driven the car for one week and owed for that amount, he could not use the car until the bill was paid. No additional negotiations concerning the use of the family car were allowed. "However," his father suggested, "there are perhaps other ways to get to the practice session." Vance did not ask his mother to override the decision. He knew that the parents would support each other. He had understood his options before he made his choice to attend the concert. He was responsible for solving problems which he created. His parents did not lecture him on his choices. They had not been involved in his earlier choices and they did not get involved in finding alternatives. He knew that they were there if he sought their advice, and of course, he could seek help from the family council. His parents recognized that they could not live his life, and while they approved of his band participation, his responsibility was to manage his resources so that this activity would have priority on his time and money. By making his earlier choice to participate in band, he had set that as a priority. No one feels sorry for him because they all have to make choices and everyone has limited resources. The distribution of resources has been fair and equitable. They assume that a sixteen-year-old is fairly realistic and relatively independent of parental control. They are good models of responsible adults and parents. They are letting him suffer the predictable consequences of his own choices.

Through their words and actions, Vance's parents communicate that all members of the family are equally important. This includes children and parents. They also believe and communicate that if one member takes more than his/her share, then someone else, or everyone else, must suffer. They act as if each person is capable of living responsibly in the family unit, and that the members are interdependent. From their attitude, clearly they do not believe that the world owes anyone a livng, but that everyone works to earn the rewards they desire. Responsibilities in the family are not determined by sex, but by interest, desire and ability. Children from this family learn how to live effectively in a relatively free environment where few controls exist. They will be able to function effectively in a democratic society. They will understand the predictable outcomes of the social system and they will be much more successful than Art will be in the competition of resources.

Human behavior is mostly learned. Individuals learn how to act by acting. Children learn what behavior works for them by trial and error. All of the people making up the family constellation—parents, cousins, aunts, grandparents, and so forth—help to determine the child's behavior. We are who we are because of our interactions.

Interactions in the family are perceived by its members as being approving (perceived as reward), disapproving (perceived as punishment), or unimportant (usually perceived as no judgment but is effective in extinguishing behavior). The most important people in one's early life are one's parents, siblings and other near-at-hand individuals whose opinions are valued. Sociologists refer to these important people as the significant others. Through our interpretations of what significant others think about us we develop our own self-images. In a sense, significant others are our mirrors, and in these mirrors we see our reflections. We act the way we think the person who is reflected should act. If we see ourselves loved and approved, we respond lovingly and with trust. If we see disapproval and rejection, we validate those perceptions through our behavior. We are what we believe about ourselves, and we develop these beliefs from the way others respond to us. The responses we get from our children are to a great extent what they think we expect from them. In a sense, our children are what they believe we think they are.

Since our parents have such an impact on our self-perceptions, a great help would be for us to choose parents who inculcate the notion that we are competent, caring and responsible. But we can't choose our parents. Also, sometimes because of our immaturity—or some other reason—we aren't the kind of parents we want for our children. This is especially true when one marries young and has children early. With the second marriage one has that unique second chance to develop the kind of family social system that enhances growth. The situation is almost like having the opportunity to choose one's own parents. We can be the kind of parents we want our children (and stepchildren) to have.

If the partners have unresolved problems themselves, a second marriage will certainly not resolve them.

The steps and procedures for accomplishing this fully-functioning healthy family system should be planned prior to the second marriage. The necessary first step is for the partners to agree on the kind of family system they want. If the partners have unresolved problems themselves, a second marriage will certainly not resolve them. If anything, a marriage will magnify problems. A healthy family requires healthy parents as models. A family can tolerate some disruptive behavior in children and can help correct such behavior if parents are healthy models and if each person in the group has something positive to offer. The parents, as leaders, are the major influences in the group. If both parents are good models and are together in terms of what they want for their family, the second marriage will offer more foundation for success.

Once a couple has decided that they want to develop a healthy family system, the next step is to resolve any differences they have concerning child guidance. Much helpful material can be found in textbooks and in the popular press. Assistance can also be obtained through formal classes and group training sessions, and through informal discussions with friends. If one has not received any help or training on parenting, he/she will be the kind of parent modeled at home. In other words, the female will replicate her mother's behavior and the male will replicate his father's mode of dealing with the family.

110

Brian and Bess typify this pattern of behavior. While they complained angrily about their parents and the way they were treated as children, they are repeating the pattern in their own lives and with their own child. **Brian**

Bess

Brian and Bess were both reared in a large family where the mother was the controlling parent. Both mothers complained about their fate. They talked about how difficult being a mother was when the mother had to be the one to make the decisions. The mothers were the ones who interceded with the father for their children when they wanted something or had a problem. The mothers were the individuals who most often spoke for the family in any sort of confrontation.

Brian and Bess both complained about their mothers. They also sympathized with their mothers who they believed suffered from "having to assume" responsibilities for the family. They both thought their mothers were domineering, which they thought was basically ineffective. Yet, Brian is the passive one in their family. Brian and Bess spend little time talking. Bess issues orders for everything from what the children will wear, when and where things will be done, to how the last dollar is to be used. Brian seems to be on the defensive and finds the act of explaining his behavior necessary. He spends a great deal of unnecessary time at his office to avoid being home. Bess fluctuates between manic and depressive stages. The children are in constant fear of displeasing their mother. They can hardly wait until they are old enough to leave home. The children's complaints about their parents sound amazingly similar to those voiced by Brian and Bess about their parents!

Effective parenting behavior can be learned and training is available in every community. This training should be accomplished prior to a second marriage since members of the second family are "ready made" and the couple must, of necessity, work with the strengths and weaknesses of those family members. Getting started on the right foot is important.

Communication between partners is the crucial component, before and after marriage, for making the family system work and keeping it working. Our society is too prone to action for many of us to have acquired effective communication skills. Because one *assumes* another individual means something does not make the point so! We can never truly know another person unless we spend adequate time communicating with that person in order to know what the individual

111

wants, feels and means. Sometimes, words do not mean the same to two different people. The word "family," for example, may mean father, mother and child to one person. To another the word might mean father, grandmother and self. To someone else, the meaning could take still some other meaning. Family is a psychological construct which we develop from our own unique set of experiences. Our experiences influence the meaning we attach to words.

Even gestures do not mean the same to different people. Visiting in Rio de Janerio, I experienced a situation in which my non-verbal behavior was misunderstood. A hand gesture, intended to communicate that the service was superb, was used. The surprised reaction brought forth the explanation that that particular gesture had a vulgar connotation. Frequent examples of words and gestures understood only by youth or by some other sub-culture often occurs. I don't believe we can assume we understand one another until we have taken time to enter into a sustained dialogue with that person. Too few couples spend enough time talking and sharing to really understand each other.

Since part of what we hear and see is dependent upon our own unique set of experiences, obviously two individuals do not automatically know what the other is saying or meaning. In a family developed from a second marriage the chances of misunderstanding are multiplied by the number of people involved. On the other hand, the opportunities for learning and expanding one's skills for communicating are expanded in direct proportion to the number and diversity of the family group. The effective use of individual and family differences was experienced by the Purcells when spending their first Christmas together.

The first time that Christmas plans were discussed in the Purcell home the children were a world apart. Jim and his children were a world apart. Jim and his children had been ac- **Carla** customed to a private midwinter vacation during the **and** Christmas season; whereas Carla and her children were **Jim** accustomed to a traditional family gathering at the grand- **Purcell** parents. Both sets of children thought their own method of celebrating the season was "the only way!" Jim's children referred to the family visit as "boring" and Carla's children thought a skiing trip was insensitive. Everyone expressed opinions and feelings. Everyone learned that other ways exist for doing things—no right and wrong way to spend Christmas exists. With a little planning and a lot of dialogue, they learned to appreciate each other's point-of-view and were able to incorporate both concepts into the season's plans. All of the family members benefitted from the experiences.

A lot of talk is necessary to understand another's point-of-view because perceptions are influenced by values, feelings and beliefs. No two people would rank all values alike and in turn do not believe the same things. As long as two people recognize that their views are different and that neither is "right" or "wrong" or even "better than," then with careful attention the two can understand and appreciate each other.

Every family needs time for conversation and sharing.

Every family needs time for conversation and sharing. This sharing time can follow the evening meal. In my family we find that this is an ideal time to share. We have set aside at least an hour when we can solve problems, talk about our successes and failures, and get opinions and data. If we have guests, they are invited to join the group, but the "family hour" takes place and takes precedence over almost all other activities. All of us value this time together, and no member of the family is absent if an absence can be avoided.

A family needs a lot of time to talk and they also need to do many other activities together. Some activities families can enjoy are: picnics, short car trips, camping, active games which involve new skills (the family members can teach others), family study groups (topics depend on group interest), and involvement in political campaigns, religious movements and social organizations. Seemingly we think of organizing groups for such purposes as these, but seldom do we think of involving our own family as a group for such activities. Our assumption is that the more of these kinds of activities we can be involved in together, the better we will understand each other, the more we will help each other and, therefore, the more cohesive will be the family system. An effective family system is a powerful personal support system. With good personal support the individual develops a strong concept of self or high self-esteem. Few families achieve maximum or near maximum effectiveness. Many families are dysfunctional.

For new parents (i.e., step parents) to be good parents and not attempt to manipulate the children in an effort to gain acceptance is sometimes difficult. A tendency exists for the new parent to want to coddle the child, to attempt to appease and thus gain favor. However, manipulative behavior is destructive, both in terms of child guidance and for one's own feelings of adequacy. If one is aware of this tendency, one will not easily succumb to the impulse. If the children are in the home only for visiting periods, both parents have to be doubly cautious to be natural and even-handed. In no sense should children be treated as guests during these visits. Instead, they should be incorporated into the family system as naturally as possible. They should, of course, participate in the family council or "family hour," and should also participate in all appropriate decision-making sessions. The "visiting" family member should share in the problem decisions as well as the non-problem decisions. Several methods can be used to make the transition of visiting in a family easier. Perhaps the child who is there for a brief time could share a room with a brother or sister. The temporary child can have responsibilities which he/she is expected to assume when in the "second" home. The parents can have certain things (such as clothes) reserved for the child to be used when he/she visits and each family member, including the one who comes only for "visits," has his/her own private area (such as chest of drawers or trunk) which is off limits to all other family members.

A child in the custody of another parent, but with frequent visits in the home, can put a strain on family relationships if agreements concerning parental roles and responsibilities are not reached. The lack of full-time responsibility does not minimize the importance of the time the parent and step-parent have with the child. Again, I would stress the urgency of reaching agreement about parenting techniques *prior to* the second marriage. Planning is required. This role is certainly too important to leave to chance.

I cannot over-emphasize the need to communicate and to have mutual goals for the family and unerring support of each other. These three factors will help to guarantee the successful development of a cohesive family, regardless of the number of individuals making up the social system. Parenting is a role which many find difficult and few have adequate training and knowledge to do effectively. But parenting can be learned and constructive behavior can be developed. A second marriage is a second chance to make that new family a healthy social system. The second marriage is also an opportunity to repeat past mistakes and to multiply errors. Step-parent stories, jokes, and ideas which have found their way into our culture imply that many second marriages are indeed disappointing and destructive. "Treated like a stepchild" is one example. A "red-headed stepchild" is apparently more suspect. The fairy tales we heard as children painted the stepmother as cruel and wanting more for "her" children than for her stepchild. Numerous stories have been written using the theme of the stepfather sexually abusing his daughter. Teachers often imply that a child is having problems because of a step-parent.

I said earlier that to be able to choose our parents would be advantageous. We can not do that, but, if we are planning a second marriage, we can certainly plan the kind of parents our children and step-children will have and the kind of social family system we will build. We can change the cruel step-parent idea of society by performing the parenting role with excellence. The family system is a social system. Since the family system is a social system, it can be engineered to meet desired goals.

ACTIVITIES FOR INDIVIDUALS AND FAMILIES

To Be Completed Following Reading of Chapter 5

Topic A—IDENTIFYING AND UNDERSTANDING ECCENTRIC BEHAVIOR.

Activity 1. Review Worksheet 5.1 which is a sample worksheet showing Eccentric Behavior Analysis of a problem with Bobby. SAMPLE: Bobby - age 7

WORKSHEET 5.1.—Eccentric Behavior Analysis

---

1. What is the misbehavior which occurs frequently? (Describe specific incident).

   Bobby will not get up in the morning. Every morning the same

   behavior occurs. He will not get up.

2. When this occurs, what do you do? How do you respond to that specific incident?

   I (mother) call Bobby two or three times—and threaten him with,

   "This is the last time!" Then dad makes a noise—like he is heading

   for the stairs—and then Bobby yells, "I'm up!"

3. What do you think and feel when this incident occurs?

   Well, I'm annoyed at first—then I get angry. He is cute the way he

   jumps up. I guess I'm aggravated and think that someday he'll learn

   and I won't have to keep reminding him!

116

4. What is the child's reaction to your response? What does the child do after you have responded to his/her negative behavior?

He gets up—comes to breakfast—he eats.

5. Then what: What do you do? What do you think?

I get his breakfast—and think, "It's about time! You are old enough to get up without being called."

6. What negative **consequence** does the child suffer from his/her misbehavior?

None. He gets his breakfast and he also gets called two or three times every morning.

7. What "eccentric behavior" did he learn from his parents' behavior? What were his/her pay-offs (positive rewards)?

He learned that parents don't really mean what they say. He learned he can get attention by being reluctant to do what he was told. He probably learned that mothers (females) are pretty helpless—and that fathers (males) are to be feared.

Activity 2. Use Worksheet 5.2 to conduct an analysis of negative or disruptive behavior which occurs regularly in your home. Fill out each blank before proceeding to the next one. For a completed sample worksheet, showing a problem with Bobby, refer to Worksheet 5.1 in Activity 1.

WORKSHEET 5.2—Eccentric Behavior Analysis

---

1. What is the misbehavior which occurs frequently? (Describe specific incident).

   _____

   _____

   _____

2. When this behavior occurs, what do you do? How do you respond to that specific incident?

   _____

   _____

   _____

3. What do you think and feel when this incident occurs?

   _____

   _____

   _____

4. What is the child's reaction to your response? What does the child do after you have responded to his/her negative behavior?

   _____

   _____

5. Then what: What do you say? What do you think?

_____

_____

_____

6. What negative **consequence** does the child suffer from his/her misbehavior?

_____

_____

_____

7. What "eccentric behavior" did he learn from his parents' behavior?
What were his/her pay-offs (positive rewards)?

_____

_____

_____

Activity 3. Apply the concept of human engineering to the story of
Trudy presented in Situation 1. Read the story of Trudy and respond to
the questions. Identify the responses which produce **Eccentric
Behavior** and/or teach **Predictable Consequences.**

SITUATION 1: Trudy

This story is about Trudy who is ten years old.

Trudy hung up the phone. She was so happy. Her best girl friend
had invited her to a spend-the-night party on Friday night. And they
had agreed on a "dutch treat" movie. She knew she would be
allowed to go! She could hardly wait to tell her family because they
wanted Trudy to have fun with her friends. But then she remembered—

she had spent all of her allowance for the whole week.

"Oh, I wish I had not spent all of my money at the fair!" she kept repeating as she tried to think what to do.

A. If you were Trudy's parents, what would you do?

_____

_____

B. What do you think Trudy might do?

_____

_____

C. What should Trudy's parents do to teach **Predictable Consequences?**

_____

_____

_____

D. Examine your response to question 1. Would your response to Trudy's problem teach her **Predictable Consequences** or **Eccentric Behavior?**

_____

_____

_____

Activity 4. If your response in Activity 3, Situation 1, question 4, would teach **Eccentric Behavior,** role play with your spouse the situation and try out other responses you might make to Trudy. Following each role-play situation, discuss the behaviors and the responses given. Also, practice (through role playing) new responses to situations you have identified (Worksheet 5.2) and the example situation of Bobby (Sample Worksheet 5.1).

HELPING CHILDREN MAKE BEHAVIORAL CHANGES.

Activity 1. Review Worksheet 5.3 which is a sample worksheet showing a problem with Allen applied to the Six Steps to Behavioral change. SAMPLE: Allen—age 9

WORKSHEET 5.3—Six Steps to Behavioral Change

Step 1. Make a clear statement about the behavior you want changed.

Allen wets the bed almost every night about midnight. I do not

want him to wet the bed at all.

Step 2. Hold a private conference with the child. *Explain* the reason for your concern about the behavior. *Listen* to the child's reason for the behavior and the problems, if any, it is causing him. *Accept* the child's perceptions as valid, and point out how you see the behavior.

Reasons: No medical reason for problem. Creates odor. Disrupts parents' sleep. Disrupts Allen's sleep. Embarrassing to Allen when he has friends in.

Step 3. *Develop* a plan for changing the behavior. Change your own (i.e., the parents) behavior which encourages the *Eccentric Behavior.* Develop new responses to reinforce *Predictable Consequences.* Decide the length of time the plan will be tried. (Suggestions for the plan should come from the child and the parents).

a) Allen will not drink water after 7 p.m. b) Allen will change his own behavior—1) do not wake up parents, 2) use only dim light (no noise), and 3) prepare clean sheets before retiring.

121

c) Allen will not look at "scary" TV programs just before bed-time. Instead, I (or my spouse or both of us) will read to Allen, a story or part of a book, just before he goes to bed. d) Length of period the plan is to be tried: two weeks.

Step 4. Follow up on the plan daily.
a) Respond (reward) to the positive behaviors.

Tell Allen how much I enjoyed sharing the story with him; help Allen make his bed.

b) Ignore (extinguish) negative behaviors and allow the child to experience **Predictable Consequences.**

Remind Allen to wash his dirty bed clothes. Have Allen clean mattress, freshen room, and so forth as needed. Do not comment about disruption at night—do not get up.

Step 5. Assess progress at specified time periods.
a) Evaluate what happened.
b) Make new plan—offer new suggestions.
c) Set new time goals.

Allen has been successful. He has not wet the bed at all for seven days and only two times the previous week. We do not feel we need to change the plan.

Step 6. Thank child for cooperation and willingness to work on the plan. Discuss how his/her and your lives are different with the behavior change.

Thank Allen for pleasant and cooperative attitude. My life is different since I am not interrupted at night; the room smells

fresh and clean. Allen is free to have friends spend the night

with him. _____

Activity 2. Use the six steps (Worksheet 5.4) as a guide for helping children make behavioral changes without punishment. Take a behavior of a child that you believe needs to be changed and apply the six steps. Write the information on worksheet 5.4. For a sample Worksheet, showing a problem with Allen, refer to Worksheet 5.3 in Activity 1.

WORKSHEET 5.4—Six Steps to Behavioral Change

Step 1. **Make** a clear statement about the behavior you want changed.

_____

_____

_____

Step 2. **Hold** a private conference with the child. **Explain** the reason for your concern about the behavior. **Listen** to the child's reason for the behavior and the problems, if any, the behavior is causing him. **Accept** the child's perceptions as valid, and point out how you see the behavior.

_____

_____

_____

Step 3. **Develop** a plan for changing the behavior. Change your own (i.e., the parents) behavior which encourages the **Eccentric Behavior.** Develop new responses to reinforce **Predictable Consequences.** Decide the length of time the plan will be tried. (Suggestions for the plan should come from the child and the parents).

_____

_____

_____

Step 4. Follow up on the plan daily.
a) Respond (reward) to the positive behaviors.

_____

_____

_____

b) Ignore (extinguish) negative behaviors and allow the child to suffer *predictable consequences.*

_____

_____

_____

Step 5. Assess progress at specified time periods.
a) Evaluate what happened.
b) Make new plan—offer new suggestions.
c) Set new time goals.

_____

_____

_____

Step 6. Thank child for cooperation and willingness to work on the plan. Discuss how his/her and your lives are different with the behavior change.

_____

_____

Activity 3. Establish a discussion period (family hour or family council) at a time convenient to the entire family. This discussion period is most effective if it occurs on a daily basis. Only a few rules should be established, and these are primarily for the purpose of encouraging members to share their concerns, successes, and disappointments, and to raise questions about others' activities. The parents should model acceptance and caring. Most responses should be reflective of the underlying feeling (see Chapter 4, Activities for Individuals and Families, for example).

Some of the general rules which might be discussed and adopted during the first session are as follows:

1. Everyone will be present and stay for the entire period. Unavoidable absences should be reported as soon as possible so that alternate plans for the discussion period can be made.

2. Every person will be given an opportunity to speak to every topic. After general discussions, the "round robin" technique (i.e. each person responds in sequence according to seating) might be used to summarize perceptions and personal positions on each topic.

3. Concensus will be reached when appropriate and if possible. Parents will not use the discussion period to give instructions, punish nor exert power.

4. Any topic is appropriate. If the amount of information is limited that others are willing to share, then they will state this without apology. Coersion will not be used to gain information.

5. What is said in the group is confidential unless permission is granted to make it otherwise.

6. The person being addressed is referred to by name and no one will talk *about* a person who is absent. Parents will model this behavior.

7. Parents will *own* and *accept* their own feelings, prejudices and ideas, and grant that permission to every member of the family. Individual differences will be *expressed* and *accepted.*

Many topics are appropriate to the discussion period. Some of the most obvious are as follows:

1. Allowances
2. Housekeeping responsibilities
3. School activities
4. Time budgets
5. Requests of parental time and assistance
6. Developmental tasks/concerns
7. Dating—boy/girl relationships
8. Moral standards and issues
9. Smoking, drugs, drinking, and so forth
10. Special recognitions (example—everyone has a special day or week)
11. Vacation
12. Problems at school
13. Religion
14. Grandparents and other relationships
15. Job changes, moves, economic issues
16. Resource allocations
17. After school jobs
18. Career planning, military

CHAPTER 6

DIVORCE PROCESS AND REDEFINITION

Culturally speaking, second marriages evolve from the failure of first marriages. However, all marriages which fail do not end in divorce and all divorces certainly do not represent personal failure. In many situations divorce facilitates personal definition and expressions of automony and strength. The situation of Julie and Harry helps one to understand how marriages can change as individuals seek to meet personal needs. As changes occur, the result may or may not be divorce. Many factors will come into play and many changes will occur when a couple experiences interpersonal problems and marriage dissatisfaction. A decision to stay married may simply be a choice not to get a divorce. Such a choice might not involve a decision to develop a more satisfying relationship nor show any concern for personal effectiveness.

Harry and Julie were high school sweethearts. When they were in their early twenties they married and in four years produced two healthy children. They were typical middle-class parents. Harry often worked overtime at the plant because he enjoyed earning the high wages paid under his union contract. He *Harry* *Julie* was a foreman and well liked by the men. The family enjoyed camping together. In the community they enjoyed participating in the neighborhood Saturday afternoon beer-and-football get-togethers.

They were good managers; thus, they had few money worries. So Julie never worked—she didn't want to work and Harry did not expect her to do so. Everything was fine between them *until. . .*

When Jeff, the oldest, was six Harry began taking him to Sunday School and occasionally staying for church. Julie was not interested in church so she stayed at home with the baby, did the household chores, and prepared dinner. For several months this seemed to be an ideal arrangement, *until* the church activities began to be more and more the central part of Harry's life. He became involved in church-related work, and soon began to insist that Julie participate in the church work also. Church socials took the place of community socials, and church outings began to substitute for camping. Their friends changed. Harry had a new commitment.

Before long, Harry informed Julie that he had been "called to the ministry" and that he had decided to respond to that calling. He told her that he anticipated being in a position to devote full time to the church within two years. He felt that within two years he could quit his job at the plant and pastor a church. He said that he would begin taking college courses in the evening immediately—or as soon as he could be accepted into the local college—and complete his college work as a student minister. He told her that this would mean financial hardships for the family, but he felt they could survive. "With God's Help" he was sure they could—and would.

Julie is frightened and angry. She is frightened because she does not know what role she is to play in this new life she is to assume—as the wife of a minister. She is angry because this is not the man she married. She married an hourly worker who was ambitious and aggressive; not a staid professional involved in serving a ministry. She is frightened and angry because she is not sure what Harry meant when he said he has been "called" to the ministry, and she is confused about why this should be so. She does not know how to discuss her confusions and frustrations with Harry, and so she keeps her own counsel. Nevertheless, she has begun to feel differently about him and their relationship. She feels she is being treated unfairly.

With his new interest and involvement, Harry does not have the time and inclination to pursue his usual recreational activities and friendships. He is too tired and too busy for camping; he is too involved with his new concerns for television watching and beer drinking. His old friendship ties have been broken, and he spends less and less time talking with Julie and sharing his dreams and plans with her. His new commitments do not seem to leave room for Julie. His new dedication is total and all consuming.

Julie suffers the stereotyped housewife syndrome. She defines herself in terms of who her husband is, and this is closely tied to his occupational title. A change in his career means a redefinition of who she is. She is not sure she can respond to the expectations people will have of her as a minister's wife. Their expectations assume she shares her husband's mission and calling. This means an independent commitment which she does not feel.

Earlier in their marriage Julie and Harry shared a compatible life space and they did not disturb each other's notions and beliefs. Through a process of events and decisions Harry has kept pushing at the edges of his comfort zone and expanding his life space. Harry's life space has come to be incompatible with Julie's life space, and in that sense they have become strangers. Conceptually, we can depict the change as is illustrated in Figure 6.1.

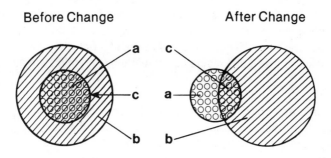

Figure 6.1. Life Space Conceptualization: (a) Julie's (b) Harry's, and (c) Overlapping.

In Figure 6.1 Julie was comfortable in a life space which was totally shared by Harry. Julie did not share all of Harry's life space (ideas, needs, etc.) but Harry shared all of Julie's life space. Their life spaces were only slightly different.

As Harry pushed at the edges of his comfort zone (e.g., trying out new ideas, beliefs, ways of doing things) and found success and support in his church, he began to expand his concept of his life space. These experiences were Harry's and were not shared by Julie. To the contrary, Julie became less communicative, more frightened and less open to new experiences. Since she did not change, their life space became incompatible.

Harry had a powerful experience in his conversion and "calling." Like most people, the very intensity of the feeling made him believe in its truth and goodness. He did not question the validity of this intense feeling because he is basically other directed or externally controlled, that is, he feels that he has little power over his own destiny but that some other force (like God) or other persons control his fate. He perceives he has little power to change how Julie feels about his choices. Although he feels his marriage is a burden at this time he also assumes that everything will work out all right. If he could not believe that everything will work out all right then he could not believe he was called to the ministry: he would feel too guilty and too unworthy.

Since Julie does not separate who she is from who Harry is, she does not perceive she has any control over her own fate either. She is not proactive; she is reactive. She will not say, "I shall do thus and so. . .," instead, she says, "what could I have done?" or "what did I do wrong?" She believes that if she *reacts* correctly then everything will be all right.

Julie and Harry both are good students of our culture. They both accepted the lessons that were taught. First Julie has bought into the manipulative playmate attitude as a girl and the reactive piggyback attitude as a wife. Harry, on the other hand, has bought into the attitude that a powerful experience is its own validity and to make a vocational decision based upon this is a man's prerogative.

The concept one has of one's self influences one's behavior. Julie judges herself harshly as basically insignificant and all messages are filtered through that lens. Julie does not express her feelings (perhaps she does not recognize nor own them), but she believes she is responsible for the behavior of others. She tries to improve the situation by "fixing" herself: she tries to change to be what the other person wants or needs. Since she is a "piggybacker" she isn't defined separately from the relationship, and since she is defined as part of Harry she cannot work with him. She can only react to him. In other words, she can be hurt with him but she cannot assist him.

Harry's world is fuzzy because he does not define where he is now nor where he wants to go. Since his world is fuzzy he believes someone—or some force—controls him. He filters all of his messages through this lens and interprets his lack of choice as his lack of control. He does know what he wants from Julie or his marriage. Therefore, Julie can never respond effectively to Harry because with ambivalence any response is partly wrong.

Their marriage will not improve if left unattended. Unlike an illness, a relationship does not heal with time. Relationships are dynamic and are in a constant state of change. Unattended, time alone can destroy a relationship. One does not establish a relationship and expect it to remain forever as it is in that moment.

Since Julie and Harry are externally controlled, for them to confront their problem is difficult. They make a **choice** not to make a choice or decision. They do not recognize this as a choice. In other words, the leave problems unresolved, thinking they are leaving to "fate" the determination of the course they will take.

Many people react in this manner. The high school student who invariably blames the "bad teacher" for his poor grades is reflecting such an attitude. So is the man who reports he is always getting short changed in the promotion department because "the boss is afraid of compet-tition." The externally controlled individual does not recognize and own his/her feelings.

One evidence of a healthy fully-functioning individual in a marriage or family is the person who shows willingness and encouragement to ask questions. Through questions one confronts one's self and others. Through confrontation one learns to appreciate who one is and who the other people are. The young child is taught or told who one is, what values to hold, and what one should think is good. With youth comes the need to examine these values. One begins to question who one really is: whether one's unquestioned values are the ones that will be consciously chosen or if other ways and ideas are better. With adulthood and maturity the confrontations seem to be between one's self and culture. This confrontation is ongoing and constant. As the mature adult moves through the adult developmental stages he/she confronts a new and changing culture and keeps negotiating with the environment. The fearful individual cannot do this. Fearful individuals look for the answer, not questions, and they refuse to recognize the changing world.

Individuals like Harry and Julie face difficulties in self awareness. They do not ask questions. Harry has difficulty because he looks to others to provide stability and security, and **Harry** Julie has difficulty because she looks to Harry for stability **Julie** and security.

To predict what will eventually happen to Julie and Harry is difficult. Possibly the two of them will stay together and ignore and live with their problem. Like Johnny and Irene, they **Johnny** may stay together for the children or for Harry's work or **Irene** because Julie cannot manage by herself. If they stay together and do not solve their problems, their growth will be **Harry** limited and, therefore, they will both lose. As the relation- **Julie** ship is, they lose the joys and vitality of a satisfying relationship, and they lose the growth and excitement that comes with resolving conflict.

That they will become overtly hostile is unlikely as long as Julie blames herself for problems, and Harry blames circumstances. They might ignore their problem and respond to the symptoms by getting a divorce. A divorce might create enough self examination to initiate a change process for them individually. If self examination happens, a divorce could be helpful, but, if they change their status solely to get rid of the problem, the situation will not be improved for long. The symptom is not the illness.

Julie and Harry both recognize they have a problem even though they have not talked about it. With a little encouragement from a significant person, that is, friend, colleague, and so forth, they might seek assistance and work out a new way of relating. I believe little hope exists that they can develop new relationship patterns without some help from an objective third party—a counselor, a trained pastor, a therapist or someone else with helping skills. First, they need help in recognizing the dynamics of their interactions and then they need help in trying out new interactions. A trained helper is needed because this self-examining will be threatening and painful. Partly because Julie and Harry have learned the cultural roles so effectively, they will have trouble seeing themselves relating in new ways.

For example, if Julie decides she will relate as an equal, that is, a compeer, this behavior will be possible only if she acquires some sensitivity to her present way of manipulating her world. A compeer relationship is possible for these two people if they change their behavior and share in the decision-making process. They both will need to develop confidence in their mutual and individual abilities to control their own lives.

Harry and Julie present a rather typical problem, especially for an early or first marriage. A couple goes into a marriage contract (relationship) without proper instruction or education concerning intimate human relationships and personality dynamics and not knowing what to expect nor how to respond. Harry and Julie learned more things not to do than to do. For example, Julie had been taught that two individuals are needed to fight and that fighting is wrong. She assumes that to disagree is to fight; thus, she withdraws rather than fight. Harry had been taught that a man is responsible for the family and he believes he should be able to control his family. He assumes that to lose control is the worst possible outcome; thus, he withdraws rather than reveal that he can lose control. How much better for Julie and Harry had they learned how to share as autonomous individuals. A helpful procedure would have been for them to learn that change is inevitable, and desirable, because only with change does one grow. Individuals enter the marriage with a contract to love "forever" and fully expect that this will be so—for as long as either shall live. Seemingly one pauses for a snapshot of a relationship and then expects to live it continually.

Love is a relationship and therefore a dynamic phenomenon. To say we "fell in love" makes little sense. For some reason, we do not say "we fell in hate" or "fell in hurt." To say we "fell in love" implies we had little choice, and, therefore, we are not responsible for what has happened or will happen.

You may respond by saying that love, hate, and hurt are emotions. This is true. They are emotions which are generated in response to a relationship. We could even argue that emotions are feelings which are generated to support a decision we have already made. For example, suppose a person, whom I shall refer to here as Ellen, has decided she wants to marry a successful, good-looking catholic of Norwegian background, who is in business for himself. She goes to a party and someone points out a guy who meets nearly all of her criteria. Their eyes meet. Ellen's heart skips a beat. It's love at first sight! She moves closer and manages an introduction. You can complete the story!

Fantasies are nice, but realism soon confronts a couple. To look at romance in a non-romantic fashion prior to the marriage contract would prevent a lot of false expectations being heaped upon that marriage by one or both partners. Webster defines romance as "having no basis in fact." The exciting feelings of love or passion or romance can be enjoyed and savored if we know that the relationship is continually and forever negotiable—and the only sure thing is that we cannot keep the relationship like it is at the moment.

Sadly, but factually, all relationships must eventually end. Some important ones will be ended with the death of another person. Most of the relationships one develops are ended much earlier. In a sense, one establishes some sort of relationship (i.e., non-verbal contract) with each person he/she meets. Some are labeled friends, perhaps one or more as lovers, occasionally someone as enemy, many as colleagues, and so forth. Both individuals involved in a relationship recognize the relationship or contract and the label (such as friend) representing it. From the label, one can estimate the amount of energy needed to maintain the relationship. A lover requires more energy than a friend, and an enemy far more than a colleague. If one has "x" amount of energy to devote to all relationships, then he/she has to determine the proportion of "x" to be devoted to the satisfying and/or dissatisfying relationships. One then devotes that amount of energy necessary to maintain each relationship.

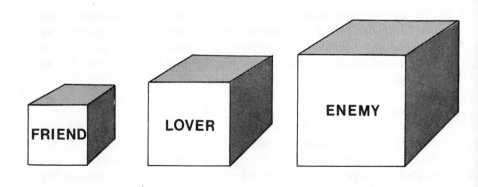

Energy requirements—"A lover requires more energy than a friend, and an enemy far more than a colleague."

You are probably thinking that one does not go through such a process. Perhaps one does not consciously go through the process, but the underlying behavior is present. One chooses his/her feelings, actions and reactions. One cannot control another's feelings, actions or reactions. Often one confuses the two and acts as though life would be beautiful if only someone else would act or do thus and so. Other people react to one according to their perception of one's expectations. The way to change the quality of the relationship is to modify one's own behavior or expectations for the relationship.

One's verbal and nonverbal behavior communicates the label placed on a relationship. One does things for friends that would not be done for colleagues, for example. Individuals are cautious around their enemies and adversaries, while being open with their lovers and buddies. Each person influences every other indiviudal with whom he/she comes into contact and is, indeed, influenced by the other person. People fashion their responses in terms of their perceptions of other's expectations and look for evidence that notions about those other persons are correct and accurate. In a sense, people are so intent on proving that their perceptions are accurate that they use energy to keep a relationship *as it is.* If the relationship is dysfunctional, energy is used to keep the relationship dysfunctional and to act as though it were a "thing apart" from the individual and unchanging and non-negotiable. One says, "Well, I wouldn't have acted that way if you had not done thus and so." But one did act that way for a purpose, that is, to keep the relationship as one has labeled it.

In a sense, a marriage contract is a formalization (or legal expression) of the relationship of two people. The marriage contract signifies that two people label their feelings and interactions as probably the most important relationship they have experienced—or expect to experience. Therefore, they wish to make a public commitment of this relationship and establish what society regards as a legally constituted and autonomous unit.

However, relationships are dynamic. That is, relationships are in a constant state of change. And so truthfully a relationship either becomes more important and more satisfying or it deteriorates. No relationship stays the same because the individuals do not stay the same. Marriage is a process. So is divorce.

Divorce is not something that happened at a given time, but over time. A relationship does not destroy an individual, but the individuals destroy the relationship. The divorce process does not alter the behavior of the participants, but it does bring into sharp focus the primary mode of relating, thinking, being; thus this change process can be used effectively as a laboratory to study and alter one's *own* behavior—but the divorce process is not a place to force another to change his/her behavior.

Many people who have experienced a divorce report that they can look back at the process and identify the major emotional steps or phases. Generally these phases were identified as (a) **Phase 1:** recognizing a problem and considering divorce as an alternative (rather than solving the problem); (b) **Phase 2:** looking to the legal system as the "only way" out of a situation that hampers another goal or commitment one or both partners have made (such as another love interest, as in the case of Johnny, or vocational goal, as in the case of Harry); (c) **Phase 3:** blaming self for mistakes and feeling worthless; and, finally, (d) **Phase 4:** redefining one's self and establishing new goals.

As I have indicated, marriage is a process and divorce is a process. *Being* is also a process. Being is a process of *becoming.* Change is the only constant thing in our society and yet one does not prepare for change. Our society does not prepare adults to confront their cultural milieu and ask hard questions about the world. Instead, people have been taught to seek security, to refrain from questions and to accept the status quo.

As has been illustrated with a number of couples, such as Karen and Jerry, and Julie and Harry, for one spouse to resist recognizing change in the other, and to deny his/her own changing attitudes and values is not unusual. To ignore change however does not mean it will go away. Probably, this means that the change will be interpreted in some fashion that is acceptable for both partners for a few months or years, and later a problem related to change will surface.

Change is gradual and consistent. A case in point is the relationship of Johnny and Irene which was discussed earlier.
They did not change all at once. Johnny did not go out   **Johnny**
looking for a new important relationship to fill some void   **Irene**
which happened when the children left home. Irene did not
make a decision one day to close Johnny out of much of her life and to turn her attention to other things and people. Seemingly the situation

"just happened" over a long period of time. Maybe one, or both, thought their mutual love for their children would somehow make the marriage work. But the parent-child relationship is not dependent on the quality of the husband-wife relationship. The marriage relationship is not even a necessary condition for the parent-child relationship. Each is separated and basically independent.

A child can never make a marriage work. A child or children may prevent the act of divorce—if we are referring to the legal act of dissolving a marriage. Instead of trying to make their marriage work, a couple should work at making the relationship satisfying.

Each relationship which is developed is based upon a set of assumptions about one's self and others which is acquired over time. For example, if a child learns to trust family members, that child will trust others who enter the home and later will trust the stranger outside the home.

Johnny and Irene could have predicted that their marriage would not be maintained after the children left home because they were both pursuing independent goals. The only common ground they had was their children. However, even with the loss of that common interest, probably they could have worked out another mutually agreed-upon goal, such a building a business together, had they been willing to face the reality of the situation and the reality of their unsatisfactory relationship. In order to maintain an existing marriage as weak as theirs, the partners would have to agree to put more energy into their relationship than would be needed for either one of them to find an alternate choice, that is, for Johnny to create a new important relationship with "Mac" or for Irene to find some cause or interest such as her family and friendship group.

When we first met Johnny and Irene, they were well into the second phase of the divorce process. They were at the point where one partner had reached the decision that "divorce is the only way" and the legal system had been called into play. Little chance exists of repairing a marriage at this stage because the personal goals of one or both parties do not include the marriage. Johnny's goals included "Mac," while Irene's primary commitment was to her family and friends. "Mac" did not "cause" the relationship to fail—even though Irene and the community blamed her for the divorce.

Energies drained from the marriage relationship do not always go into other love interest. Harry illustrates this. If we examine behavior, we will note that people put their energies into a variety of relationship activities which seems to substitute for a satisfactory marriage. The most obvious of these is a sexual relationship. While I recognize that a sexual relationship is possible without even a hint of love, much less marriage, I also believe that any energies put into such a relationship detract from the marriage relationship. Given our cultural values and attitudes, I feel that the sexual relationship should be limited to one's spouse.

Concern and involvement with the social needs of society is another substitute for one's energies which offers a high degree of satisfaction to a large segment of our society. This concern may have its basis in religious beliefs and experiences, in philosophy, or even in personal needs. For example, if the interpersonal sexual relationship is not developed, the individual may substitute societal needs or some other type of concern to fill that void. Culturally, people are taught that substitution is a good and noble way to expend their energies, so an individual is able to gain considerable recognition and "pay-off" for devotion to societial needs and this sometimes at the detriment of other people (wife or husband, for example) because such behavior leaves little time or energy for them. A glimpse of this type of situation is illustrated in the lives of Harry and Julie.

Another type of relationship which requires energy I shall label friendship. Individuals are gregarious and need the contact of other people. Persons can keep friendship at several levels, ranging from popularity to love. They also can use friendships to advance personal desires, to advance politically or economically for example, and to gain what they want. They can even simulate sexual interest and welfare concerns through friendship relationships. Yet friendship does not require the long-term commitment that married sexual love does nor the dedication and altrusion required to satisfy welfare needs. Culturally, a tendency exists to bestow individuals devoted to friendship with economic and social rewards. People are influenced by this type of individual and they tend to use him/her to influence others. Friendship-type persons are first praised and the first criticized. Maybe because they they are so clearly in the line of vision, they demand attention. If excessive energy is devoted to friendship, the other types of relationships suffer.

A less obvious but much used demand on one's energies is related to creative and intellectual pursuits. These pursuits are sometimes substitutes for warm personal human relationships. The creative person keeps searching for new forms and ways of expression. As Thoreau said, the creative person marches to a different drummer. Culturally creative persons are "forgiven" for their differences, especially if society benefits from the creative endeavors. The "star" who entertains and artists who enrich other's lives are championed. Yet, like other concerns, dedication to creative or intellectual interests takes its toll from other concerns, including sexual loves, welfare and friendships. Creative individuals are rewarded by tolerating their deviations but are punished by others failing to understand them and thereby closing them off. In a sense, the creative person is no more "different" than the organizer who works with the transient worker (welfare concerns), or the politican who influences thousands with personal contacts (friendship concerns), or the husband-lover who retreats into the wilderness to share a life of blissful togetherness with his loved ones (sexual love). In each of these examples, one type of love is so all-consuming that little or no room exists for a balance of energies going into the several areas.

Compatible couples put similar amounts of energy in the several broad types of concerns: (a) sexual, (b) welfare, (c) friendship and (d) creative.

As I tried to point out earlier, individuals have a given amount of energy to express (identified as "x") and they choose how they will distribute that energy. Compatible couples put similar amounts of energy in the several broad types of concerns: (a) sexual, (b) welfare, (c) friendship and (d) creative. The frustrated couple direct their sexual energy away from the partner and into one of the other categories. Examples are: The. . ."workaholic" who can't take time from the job to enjoy an afternoon with the spouse; a husband or wife who can't let go of the welfare concerns of some group or individual to be concerned about the sexual fulfillment of the spouse; and the scholar so busy influencing his/her public that he/she fails to notice that the spouse is begging for attention and love.

Harry and Julie are an example of a spouse redirecting his energies from that of husband (sexual) to that of the church (welfare). Irene is an example of a spouse directing her energies toward family welfare and friendship. Irene has moved in this direction over a rather extended period of time; Harry changed somewhat more abruptly. Seldom are welfare, friends, or art blamed for divorce. But to me, they seem to be as involved in the process as are love interests.

Harry
Julie

Irene

Seemingly those people whose marriage is no longer their primary relationship, but who remain married, nurse a big hurt. They are still defined as a couple but they, especially the wife, are locked into the hurt feeling. This hurt is incapacitating and limits growth. Unlike their divorced peers, no redefinition of self will take place because the definition is related to the marriage. Hurt, like anxiety, is nebulous and fuzzy and does not have a clear object on which to focus; therefore, dealing with hurt and resolving it is most difficult.

With divorce, redefinition is necessary. The couple definition is destroyed. The life space is no longer shared. But following the divorce, and prior to the redefinition when new goals are set and autonomy is achieved, most people report that they go through a period of self-doubt, self-blame, negativism and disillusionment.

The world may seem something like a stage and they are the actors—as Shakespeare noted—but for the newly divorced, no lines and no director exist. The things they once thought worked, did not; the goals they set as a couple, no longer exist. The play has to be rewritten. And to realize that the individual is the author, not someone else takes awhile. That the individual is the director, not some other being, either natural or supernatural also takes time! The individual has the arena, the parts, the script—the direction is under his/her own control. This situation is new and frightening. But what an opportunity for redefinition.

The identity of self, apart from the other (former spouse), may seem unclear to the individual in this transition period, that is, this time between the legal divorce and the period when energies can be focused upon the development of goals and the redirection of purpose. Can the divorced person use this transition period effectively and productively? The answer is a tentative "yes." The answer is tentative because seemingly the phase is necessary and little can be done to hurry through it or to not experience it at all. Even if the individual is goal directed, basically autonomous and independent, the transition period seems to be experienced. Several incidences from individual lives will help to clarify the dynamics of the transition period.

Let us examine the dynamics involved with Johnny and Irene. Irene had spent so much psychological energy, thought, and time attempting to prevent the divorce, that she was bound to suffer a feeling of deprivation or loss when the divorce was finally granted. Deprivation is a psychological state. Individuals feel deprived when they give up something they did not want to relinquish. For example, you might give your friend an evening to help him/her build a boat and feel good about the project; but, if an unwanted visitor spent the evening at your home and kept you from some enjoyable activity you had planned, you would feel deprived. In this sense, deprivation leads to anger, hurt, and frustration. To use these emotions in a productive fashion is difficult. The usual reaction is to seek revenge. Irene **Irene** uses her deprivation-related emotions to involve her **Johnny** friends and family in ways to gain sympathy for herself and antagonism or resentment toward Johnny. Until Irene realizes that Irene cannot control Johnny, but Irene can control Irene, she will use her energies in a counter-productive manner. She will stay in the transition phase until she gives up her fight for revenge. Johnny also experiences the transition phase. He has fought Irene so hard for the divorce, and then fought the criticism of the community to gain acceptance for his new wife, that he and "Mac" have developed a "we-they" position. So much of his energy had gone into protecting **Johnny** himself and "Mac" against family and friends that he has **"Mac"** little energy left to redirect his own goals. As long as he sees the two of them against the world, his behavior will be controlled by that perception. He will be reactive rather than proactive. He will remain in the transition period until he is able to establish new goals and redirect his life.

Carolyn, a nurse, didn't feel any loss at her divorce, instead she felt relief. Her husband had been abusive and tempermental displaying psychotic episodes. Yet, her transition phase was marked with some of the feelings similar to Johnny's. She had fought her husband so long and had responded to his moods so completely, that her life seemed like a large empty room without that problem. **Carolyn** She no longer had that uncontrollable monster to fight, but she had forgotten how to relate to another person in a normal give-and-take relationship. She found she actually missed the tension and fear and she wondered if she would ever be able to fill her life again. Even a burden offers a way of finding meaning. Survival can be a goal, but if survival is assured, then we ask, "What next?"

People like Carolyn, who are dealing with a void (nothing to do now, not even revenge to attempt), tend to fall back on earlier patterns of behavior to create meaning in life. This type response is expressed in a variety of ways. "I gained forty pounds after my divorce," related a successful professor, whose first marriage had been especially limiting. "He cruised around like a teenager and talked about things I was embarrassed to hear," related a young man, speaking of his newly-divorced friend. "She plunged into her work and never had time for dates!" was the way one interested male saw his friend following her divorce. Others take "extended vacations," go on drinking binges, spending sprees, and so forth. The behaviors seem purposeless and random. But during the transition phase, the individual is searching for meaning—a person in search of a goal.

Like a youth who finally gets through the teens and assumes a mature role befitting a twenty-year-old, the transition period finally, but gradually, comes to a close. This happens when the individual finally has focused his/her energies on a goal; when he/she has redirected his/her life and established new goals.

One can't search for happiness and succeed; one can search for meaning and ways to give meaning to others and perhaps find happiness as a by-product.

Many people find assistance in redirecting their lives through group or individual counseling. Some report that they found help through such groups as "Parents Without Partners," church-related or other self-help groups. Many, especially women, become involved in going-back-to-school or participating in new activity groups. Men and women report they have found personal satisfaction during this period by redirecting their energies into some short-term but meaningful project. As numerous philosophers have said, people find happiness as a by-product of some other activity. Jesus said an individual gains life by losing it. One can't search for happiness and succeed; one can search for meaning and ways to give meaning to others and perhaps find happiness as a by-product.

Even in our permissive time, few women seem to feel complete without a mate. This idea probably has its basis in the cultural expectation that the wife is the helpmate, the supporter of the doer, the one who encourages and pampers the mate who fights the economic wars and deserves being pampered. Many men still want a wife to be an attachment to them, a supplement to their career, a housekeeper and a guardian of virtues which have difficulty surviving "out there." Yet this traditional relationship, regardless of how it is romanticized in song and story, is not satisfying to most people. Men seek companionship with *equals,* (i.e., male peers) outside their home and call these relationships clubs, hunting companions, political friends, and so forth. The wife (in the traditional sense) is generally left to develop her *equal* relationship with whoever is available, such as small children, teenage sons and daughers, elderly parents, and so forth. No wonder the husband and wife have less and less in common as they live together! How noticeable this situation is when they need each other as companions, peers, and friends, as well as lover and helper.

Some people try to avoid the label (and sex-role stereotyping) by avoiding the legal act of marriage. This probably has the advantage of giving the individual the freedom to work out individual relationships. Legal problems (in dissolving the relationship, death, etc.) are encountered in these arrangements and a cultural disadvantage exists in that others do not know what label (or labels) to give the relationship. The couple's position has to be negotiated with each new encounter.

The redefinition of an individual should be complete before he/she attempts to enter into a new marriage. A marriage should be a relationship that enhances one's own goals and meets the intimate relationship needs of both partners. A second marriage is a good time to make a marriage that is not limited by sex-role expectations and not based on neurotic needs.

As I have indicated earlier, I favor the marriage of two individuals who are equal and autonomous. I call this a relationship of compeers. Compeers argue, compete, discuss, evaluate, share, and so forth. In other words, compeers are just two human beings who are united in marriage—because they like being together.

ACTIVITIES FOR INDIVIDUALS AND FAMILIES

To Be Completed Following Reading of Chapter 6

Topic A—STUDYING AND MODIFYING PROBLEMS

Activity 6.1. Each member of the family is to mark the **Problem Check-list** independently of one another. Check each item comprising each factor in one of two categories, "Like Me, Yes," or "Not Like Me, No."

PROBLEM CHECKLIST ITEMS	Like Me Yes	Not Like Me No
FACTOR A	Check One	
1. I believe I have little control over my life.	☐	☐
2. I am unhappy about my life, but I have no alternatives.	☐	☐
3. I feel I have given up a great deal for the family.	☐	☐
4. I am torn between my feelings of responsibility and what I want for myself.	☐	☐
Parent Answers: Sometimes my spouse and/or children embarrass me.	☐	☐
Child Answers: Sometimes my parent(s) and/or sibling(s) embarrass me.	☐	☐
FACTOR B	Check One	
1. I wish I could talk things over with my spouse/parent(s).	☐	☐
2. I keep secrets from my family and they keep secrets from me.	☐	☐
3. All members of my family are not treated with equal respect.	☐	☐
Parent Answers: My spouse does not understand me.	☐	☐
Child Answers: My parents do not understand me.	☐	☐

4. Some issues are not discussed in our family. ☐ ☐

FACTOR C	Check One

---

1. I am not as attractive as I believe I should be. ☐ ☐
2. I am afraid of losing love when I disagree or displease my spouse (parents). ☐ ☐
   Parent Answers: I feel important and worthwhile only in relation to my ability to be a good spouse and/or parent. ☐ ☐
   Child Answers: I feel important and worthwhile only in relation to my ability to be a good family member. ☐ ☐
3. I am not as good a person as I should be. ☐ ☐
4. If my family knew my motives, they would not think highly of me. ☐ ☐

FACTOR D	Check One

---

1. I am too settled and content to desire new and different experiences. ☐ ☐
2. I think some people throw away money on foolish activities such as travel, education and new hobbies. ☐ ☐
3. I believe a mother's place is in the home, and that a father's responsibility is to make a living. ☐ ☐
4. I think to allow children to question the values of the family is dangerous. ☐ ☐
5. I believe certain subjects should be taboo in the family discussions. ☐ ☐

Activity 6.2. After each member of the family has completed the *Problem Checklist*, then the individual is to read the "Interpretation after completing the Problem Checklist" which follows:

If you answered "yes" to one or more items on the Problem Checklist, you are probably experiencing problems and are concerned about your effectiveness in one or more of the four categories identified as Factor A, B, C and D.

Factor A is related to one's self-awareness (i.e., the willingness to **own** and **accept** one's feelings). Awareness of self represents the first step in personal development and mental health.

Factor B is related to communication. An open and accepting attitude about one's own worth is a part of accepting others. If a person feels comfortable with **who** and **what** he or she is, then that person can be comfortable with **who** and **what** another is. When one is accepting, open, and congruent, no areas are closed to communication and sharing.

Factor C is related to self-concept. A person who feels valued as a person does not have to prove his or her worth. Self-acceptance and a positive self-image are reflected in the perceptions one has of others. In other words, we see in others what we believe about ourselves.

Factor D is related to values. A person who insists that one should not question values is afraid of losing his or her meaning and sense of purpose. A person with a rigid value system uses fear and disapproval as techniques of control.

Activity 6.3. After each member of the family has completed the **Problem Checklist** and read the "Interpretation," then the individual is to read the following "Recommendations:"

A fully-functioning family, comprised of mentally healthy individuals, is a goal worthy of attention and effort. If you have answered "yes" to any of the items on the Problem Checklist, it is quite likely you could benefit from professional services to help you clarify problems and needs. Also, other approaches might be used in combination with counseling or as independent activities. All are intended to help the individual and family expand their perceptions of appropriate behavior and understand the concept of individual uniqueness. These approaches are enumerated below.

1. Family discussions (i.e., family hour or family council) are necessary to the development of healthy family interactions. A fully-functioning family cannot short circuit conversation. One gains support from others who share concerns and offer under-

standing. (See Chapter 4 Activities for ways to implement a family-discussion period).

2. Solve problems and develop concensus about issues by using the VISUAL Method (see Chapter 2 Activities for this model). No child is too young and no adult too old to learn to be effective problem solvers.

3. Develop understanding of intra-personal and inter-personal dynamics through the use of self-help materials such as *Second Marriage*. One or more couples and/or families might benefit from group discussions using such materials.

4. Develop your own plan for growth and improvment. Some activities which others have found helpful and offered as examples and suggestions.
   (a) Take courses, credit and non-credit, to develop special skills or interests.
   (b) Change jobs or family routine.
   (c) Plan and make a major trip, or some similar demanding activity.
   (d) Take a study-therapy vacation away from the children.
   (e) Become involved in a personal improvement workshop such as assertiveness training.

Activity 6.4. As a family unit discuss the problems, interpretations, and recommendations identified individually in the previous three activities. (See Chapter V Activities for ways to implement a family discussion period.)

Topic B—DEFINING AND RECOGNIZING SELF

Activity 6.5. Each member of the family individually is to use Worksheet for Activity 6.5 to make a self portrait and plan. In so doing, the individual is to make a plan for becoming the kind of person he/she wants to be.

WORKSHEET FOR ACTIVITY 6.5—SELF PORTRAIT AND PLAN

1. My name is _____

2. How I feel about my name _____

    _____

3. Three words or sentences which describe me:

    (1) _____

    (2) _____

    (3) _____

4. How I feel about the descriptive words or sentences in item 3:

    (1) _____

    (2) _____

    (3) _____

5. What I want for myself:

    (1) _____

    (2) _____

    (3) _____

6. How I plan to get what I listed in item 5:

What I Will Do	How I Will Do This	When I Will Do This
(1) _____	_____	_____
(2) _____	_____	_____
(3) _____	_____	_____

Activity 6.6. After each member of the family has completed worksheet for Activity 6.5, have a family discussion to share how the family members can help one another achieve the desired plans.

Activity 6.7. Each member of the family individually is to use Worksheet VI-B to examine the impact of his/her emotions on inter-personal interaction in problem situations.

WORKSHEET FOR ACTIVITY 6.7—PROBLEM ANALYSIS

1. Identify a problem you are experiencing.

   _____

   _____

   _____

2. Specifically, what is it about this problem which causes you concern?

   _____

   _____

   _____

3. What are you feeling about the problem? State your emotions as exactly as possible.

   _____

   _____

   _____

4. What purpose do your emotions serve? Because of these emotions, what do you do?

   _____

_____

_____

5. Who is responsible for the problem? Who are the participants?

_____

_____

_____

6. How would your life be different if you did not have this problem?

_____

_____

_____

7. What can you do to change the problem you are experiencing?

_____

_____

_____

Activity 6.8. After each member of the family has completed Worksheet VI-B, then have a family discussion to determine how family members can help each other with the problems existing.

CHAPTER 7

CREATIVE LIVING

Being and *becoming* are two words which I use frequently as I try to describe a person who is comfortable with the present and anticipating the future. Being and becoming are words I use to mean owning, accepting and liking who one is and what one is now (being) and trusting in what one will be (becoming). I have talked about the importance of owning one's feelings and behavior and separating one's self from the significant others (and things) in one's life; that is, knowing where one individual stops and another person or thing starts. Some parents, for example, cannot separate themselves from their children. A father who played football in high school insisted his son, Earl, forget band (which he loved) and play football (which he hated). This father was the mainstay for the midget team when his son was playing in that league. The father talked and stressed football constantly, and went to great trouble and expense to insure that his son played first string. When he was in high school, Earl was not a good student and he suffered from respiratory problems. Nevertheless, at his father's insistence he played football. He worked hard trying to be a good player. Following a very demanding game, which his team lost, Earl was killed in a one-car accident. The report stated that he was driving too fast for the road conditions and lost control of the car. A picture of him in his football uniform appeared in the paper. The headlines read, "Car Accident Claims Life of Football Player." I could not help but think that Earl never had a chance to be himself because his father could not separate the two of them. When Earl succeeded, his father felt elated; when Earl failed, his father was defeated.

Sometimes we confuse "things" with ourselves. A man drove his new car into the service station. He got out, patted the car, and told the attendant to "fill 'er up!" A stranger standing nearby commented, "Those new cars are really gas guzzlers." The owner went into great detail "defending" his car: it was the **best**; it could pick up speed the fastest; it was the easiest to maneuver; and so forth. The stranger would have understood the defensive response had he realized that to criticize the car was to criticize the man. The owner could not separate himself from the car!

Women, especially typical housewives, sometimes cannot separate themselves from their sex-role stereotype activities. For example, a husband sat down to the Thanksgiving dinner and criticized the way the turkey was cooked. His wife burst into tears. She somehow identified so closely with the turkey that his evaluation of the turkey became, in her mind, an evaluation of her own worth. Of course this kind of husband-wife interaction comes from relationships built on incongruent messages, manipulations, and closed-communication systems. In a similar manner, a husband or wife sometimes perceives a spouse as an accessory or an extension of his or her professional role or social status. Jim represented this kind of confusion when he did not want Diane to go with him to the class reunion because she did not know how to dress. He would be embarrassed.

I have tried to make clear that human beings, while unique, have a great deal in common, and that human-ness is all that is expected of any of us.

I have tried to make clear that human beings, while unique, have a great deal in common, and that humanness is all that is expected of any of us. We get into problems, psychologically speaking, because we expect too much of ourselves and of others. These great expectations we hold are based on some belief that others control our lives, or that we have to live up to what others want us to be like. If one is busy trying to please others, he/she will be self-conscious and uncomfortable with what he/she is and confused about what he/she wants to become. Each individual is responsible for his or her own behavior and feelings. What one believes about others' expectations are actually projections of what one believes about one's self. Pretending to live up to the expectations of others is to deny one's own responsibility.

The mental exercises which follow will help you see that you can control your feelings:

(a) Close your eyes. Think about yourself. (How do you feel? What is the environment like: the temperature, the smell, the sounds? Are you comfortable?) Open your eyes. Describe how you feel.

(b) Close your eyes again. Think about some favorite place and time when your world is the happiest. (What is it like being there: the temperature, the sounds, the smells? How do you feel?) Open your eyes. Describe how you feel.

(c) Compare the two. Were your feelings different? Who controlled those feelings?

One chooses one's feelings in a situation as surely as one chooses the situation. As I have suggested previously, one generates feelings to obtain momentum to do whatever is desired or wanted. If a spouse wants to fight, for example, then he/she generates feelings of anger, hurt, pain, and so forth. If a person wants to love another, one generates feelings of caring, excitement, identity.

To try to control others is useless because one can only control one's self. Therefore, the place to start in partnership development is with one's own feelings, actions, and reactions. While sounding like a paradox, personal independence is necessary before a healthy dependent relationship can be developed with another. Prior to a second marriage is a psychologically sound time to develop autonomy, to understand one's own goals and to prepare one's self to be a strong supportive spouse. The expectations one has of others is directly related to one's self expectations. We are afraid of a weakness in others which we fear in ourselves. Accepting and being comfortable with a spouse is directly related to one's own feelings of adequacy or inadequacy.

These next activities help you examine what you expect from yourself. Clarifying what you expect from yourself gives you an idea about how you expect to be treated by others.

153

Activity 7.1. First, in the blanks below, write three adjectives which you feel describe you and then complete the sentence using the adjective. For example, I might write: **Thoughtful.** I am a **thoughtful** person.

Adjectives   Sentences

1. _____ I am a (an) _____ person.

2. _____ I am a (an) _____ person.

3. _____ I am a (an) _____ person.

Activity 7.2. Your parents, mother or father, probably would describe you as _____(fill in adjective). Your husband/wife or best friend would probably say you are_____(fill in adjective). Is either of the adjectives idential to the ones you used to describe yourself in Activity 7.1? Probably so. Most of us are still seeing ourselves like our parents saw us—regardless of our age.

Activity 7.3. Now go back to the three adjectives you wrote in Activity 7.1 about yourself. Circle the adjective which is the most descriptive of yourself.

Activity 7.4. Now, consider the word you circled. Decide how much of the time that word describes you by drawing a box around one of the following: Almost Always, Most of the time, Occasionally.

I shall refer to this box (Activity 7.4) later and you will use the word in a later exercise, but for now, let us examine what Rachael wrote about herself.

Rachael, (whom you met briefly in Chapter 1), describes herself as **outgoing, helpful, conforming.** She grew up in a family comprised of a mother, father, older sister, and younger brother. Her maternal grandmother lived next door. She believed she was grandmother's favorite. Rachael felt her older sister was the **Rachael** apple of her father's eye, and that her younger brother was the favorite of the mother. She resented her sister but she did not resent her brother so much since he was the "only boy" and this made him "special." She felt she had to work hard to gain recognition and attention. She received attention by being more helpful around the house than her sister, more clever than either her brother or sister, not causing any trouble, and being Grandmother's helper. She usually returned from school with some exciting incident to tell which would capture the family's attention. She proved she was clever: she memorized all sorts of materials (poems, sayings, etc.) and used these to impress the family. She felt she was a lot better at school work than her brother and that she caused a lot less trouble at home than her sister. Her evaluation of her sister was that she was "downright selfish."

Rachael remembers that when she was a child if she was not feeling up to par, or was unhappy about something, or was worried, her brother or sister or someone would say to her, "Rachael, what's wrong? You're not yourself today." Or her mother would say, "Smile, Rachael, you're not supposed to be in a bad mood!" Also, she recalls that her mother would comment, "Let Rachael help with that (housework or whatever)," and her Grandmother would add, "Yes, Rachael is always so helpful. I don't know what I would do without Rachael—Grandmother's Helper!"

Rachael felt good when she was praised. As a child, when people told her she was not acting like herself, she would try to change her mood or behavior to conform to their expectations. Now she is a grown woman expecting to get married a second time, and she still sees herself as she believes her family saw her as a **Rachael** child. She is about to marry Robert, who is probably in love **Robert** with her because she is so opposite from himself. (Remember him? He is self-centered, concerned about his own needs, and unlike Rachael, does not like to be in social situations.) She is probably in love with Robert **because** she cannot be those things he is, and thus, he completes her life as surely as she completes his!

I think of Rachael as in an "Almost Always" box in terms of her behavior. She is "Almost Always" helpful. I believe that when someone is in an "Almost Always" box we can examine that person's family and find some member which that person believes to be "exactly opposite," that is, in the opposite "Almost Always" box. For example, in Rachael's family, his sister was her opposite. Rachael was "Almost Always" **helpful** and her sister was the opposite, that is, **selfish.** Now that she is no longer with her sister, she seeks that same behavior in her spouse.

The following diagram is an illustration of the kind of balance within the family which is achieved when members see their behavior limited to "Almost Always" boxes:

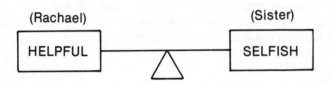

(Rachael)   (Sister)

HELPFUL   SELFISH

Figure 7.1. Rachael's Perception of Family Behavior.

Activity 7.5. Are you in an "Almost Always" box (refer to Activity 7.4)? If you are, complete the "Almost Always" family balance diagram for yourself.

(Your Name_____)   (Opposites' Name _____)

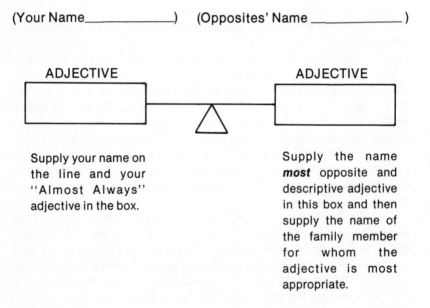

ADJECTIVE   ADJECTIVE

Supply your name on the line and your "Almost Always" adjective in the box.

Supply the name *most* opposite and descriptive adjective in this box and then supply the name of the family member for whom the adjective is most appropriate.

Figure 7.2. Perceptions of One's Own Family's Behavior.

Rachael feels she is "Almost Always" helpful and she is this way because she sees this as a way of finding her place. She is helpful so much of the time that when she is not acting that way, the significant other people won't accept her behavior. They tell her in effect, "Rachael, get in your 'Almost Always' box. That is the way you are important in this family. Rachael is supposed to be helpful. We love her when she is helpful!"

Rachael disregards any information concerning herself which does not conform to this perception. If she is not helping at all—or does not want to help—she ignores that action or feeling. When her sister is more helpful that she, she resents that behavior or ignores it because being helpful is her prerogative. A more objective evaluation convinces us that everyone, including Rachael's sister, is helpful sometime (or wants to be) and that everyone, including Rachael, is not helpful at times (or does not want to be). However, if Rachael believes she is not "Almost Always" helpful, she will have to do away with the "Almost Always" box and lose her place. If she changed her perceptions of herself she would have to change her perceptions of her sister also. The more we understand and accept ourselves, the more we are willing to accept a wide range of behavior as appropriate for ourselves and for the significant other people around us. In other words, the more we accept ourselves, the more we accept others.

If Rachael were accepting of a wide range of behavior for herself, she would see that she has self-worth even *if* and *when* she is not helpful. She would still like herself. This might change her relationship to Robert. Robert might not want to marry her if she were different. Her "Almost Always" helpful style meets his selfish style. Nevertheless, with high self esteem, Rachael would be more comfortable with someone who could accept her *as she is.* She would not marry someone to meet her own neurotic needs—nor to meet his neurotic needs. Interestingly Robert completes a balance for her in the same way her sister did. With high self regard Rachael would not find necessary to search constantly for validation of her own worth. She would know she is of worth. As long as she is in an "Almost Always" box she will have to keep checking with significant others to see if she still has her place.

Just as Rachael resented her sister for not being helpful—or for being selfish—she will also resent Robert for that same style. And with Robert, just as she did with her sister, Rachael will think she has to be the way she is because he (Robert) will not change. She will think her "fate" is to carry the burden of being the helper, and she will keep reinforcing that behavior.

Neurotic dependency exists when an individual limits or denies part of him/herself. If one has meaning only as a part of another person, logically that individual both fears and needs the other person. A marriage between two dependent parts is not a healthy partnership. A marriage between two fully-functioning autonomous individuals, who like to be together and offer enrichment to each other's lives, is a partnership of peers. Earlier, I have referred to this fully-functioning relationship as compeers.

Many marriages, especially many first ones, seem to be of the dependent-dependent relationship type. The personal tragedy and social cost of the dependent-dependent type marriage is phe-nomenal. The story of Gayle illustrates the debilitating *Gayle* effects of this type of relationship. The story could be repeated many times with only the names changed. Society fails to prepare individuals for marriage. Perhaps in the second marriage with the individual being more mature, the couple will prepare themselves for the relationship. Never is change too late. A crisis will sometimes force growth. As we shall see, Gayle has reached a crisis. She will become more self-sufficient now or she will deteriorate and become even more dependent and incapacitated with self doubt.

Gayle, at thirty-eight, is a widow. She had been married for twenty years when Dale, her husband, was killed in a mine accident. An engineer, he was underground when an explosion occurred that took his life. Gayle was unprepared to be alone. She had never worked. She has two sons, one eighteen and a senior in high school, and the other twenty and a freshman at the State University. Gayle has been a mother and wife ever since she has been an adult. At times, she said she felt she was only a mother, that she had three boys. Her husband expected much of the mothering behavior her children received. Although Gayle was outgoing and enjoyed social contacts, she spent most her time with home activities and family. Dale hated to be in public or social gatherings. He felt a woman's place was basically in the home with the family. He provided well for the family and asked little of Gayle. He left the management of the home and children to her. He was as retiring, quiet, and methodical in the family as he was at work.

Gayle had one year of college. She met Dale during her first year on campus. When they met, he was finishing his master's degree. He told her he was responsible, mature and ready to "take a wife." Oddly enough, she recounts that she felt sorry for him for some reason, maybe because he was so thin and quiet. She remembers wondering (like a good mother) if he got enough to eat. She wanted to look after him.

They were married and she enjoyed the first few years "looking after him." He loved coming home in the evening to his "home cooked" dinners, to his wife, and to his favorite chair, with the daily paper in just the right spot. After the children were born Gayle was the one who took the boys shopping and swimming. She was the one who played with the youngsters. Gayle and the boys went to the church as a family. On several occasions Gayle had suggested to Dale that she would like to go back to school or perhaps to work. Each time, Dale discouraged her. He let her know that he felt he needed her at home, and that the boys certainly needed her there.

Gayle was ambivalent: she wanted Dale to need her, but she also felt used. (Now that he is dead, she can only remember needing him). She was obviously pleased when she told her pastor that Dale did not want her to work. But prior to his death, she had complained to her best friend that she had no life of her own. She questioned her effectiveness as a mother. She was anxious and overweight. Dale was the provider: he gave her a livelihood and made her feel needed. She resented being used by Dale, but now she feels guilty that she had those feelings. Now she hates herself for her past failures and shortcomings.

Now that Dale is dead, she is at a total loss. Her boys do not need her. They will both be away at school soon. She is not needed at home. There is no Dale to do things for.

Her pastor suggested she become involved in some project or civic activity. "You are needed," he told her. But a cause does not appeal to her. She does not know how to get involved in anything meaningful. Sometimes she thinks about marrying again, but then she feels guilty that she can fantasize "replacing" Dale so easily. She is frightened and has sought help from her pastor. She is afraid she is approaching depression and she has had thoughts of suicide. She is scared. She seems to have few personal resources or inner strengths.

Gayle is, of course, in an "Almost Always" box. She sees herself as a "mother"—someone who always "sees after" someone else. Gayle is in the "Helper" box. She is a "see after" type helper. Being a mother, she needs a child or dependent. She becomes weary of the task sometimes, but when she is without someone to look after, she feels worthless. Dale, was of course, in the helpless box. He even looked helpless. He "took a wife" to see after him. Theirs was a dependent-dependent relationship. The two of them were needed to complete one life.

If Gayle gets appropriate help, she will use this crisis to bring about a positive change in her own life, thereby becoming an effective person. Probably Gayle will not make the crucial personal changes which will bring about growth and development. Most likely she will continue to mother the boys as much as possible, and will keep searching for someone to fill the void left by Dale's death. She will not search for another person with whom to develop a mutually satisfying relationship, but will, instead, look for a substitute for Dale. Unless her pastor is perceptive concerning the dynamics of behavior, he will eulogize Dale and fail to uncover Gayle's feelings of resentment and guilt. She will keep her feelings hidden because she believes to feel the way she does is wrong. Her pastor's praise for Dale's virtues (which is a reflection of her own verbal expressions) will precipitate even greater feelings of guilt and thus even greater despair. Unless she admits her feelings, and accepts them as human emotions which must be confronted, she will not be able to resolve her problems. Gayle cannot develop feelings of self worth as long as she keeps herself in her "Almost Always" box. As long as she accepts herself only as being an "Almost Always" helper, she will not be free to examine her true feelings. She has put herself in another box. With Dale's death, she perceives that she **should** have only good feelings and appreciation for Dale. Her momentary feeling of relief and freedom upon learning of Dale's death was such a traumatic confrontation that she immediately labeled herself (not her feelings) as **bad** and **unworthy.** She felt ashamed! She felt she should be punished! Thus she went into depression and had thoughts of suicide. She cannot identify the source of her problem because she will not allow her feelings to be examined. She says, to herself and others, what she believes she should say and what she thinks they expect to hear.

As our society is becoming more permissive and open, more and more people are learning how to deal with their emotions. I am optimistic concerning our emotional ability to be more loving and less hating. I believe we will continue to help people see that an emotion or feeling is not innately wrong, and that to own feelings is far better than to deny them. I believe we are becoming more self accepting and, therefore, more tolerant of ourselves and of others.

I believe our changing attitude toward second marriage is one example of our (collective) willingness to examine ourselves and our social structure, and to make adjustments in both. Mistakes are not irreversible. If we have made an unhappy first marriage, this situation does not have to doom our second one. Behavior is resistant to change, but change is possible. Change is painful perhaps, but not unbearable. If we can learn from our errors and mistakes, we can call our errors trials, and we can call our mistakes experiences.

Gayle has attempted to substitute domesticity for love. Dale substituted physical comforts for love. Love includes caring for, but more. Love is sharing one's self. A healthy love relationship, at least in our modern society, is a compeer relationship in which both partners are equal. Being equal and important individually makes the partnership a synergistic relationship. One person does not complete another. Yet, together, they produce more than the two can produce independently. Such partners come together because they enjoy and benefit from the relationship; they do not come together in order to survive (psychologically). Second marriage happens at a time when individuals are mature enough to know what marriage is all about. They should be able to accept love and to give love because they are not afraid of their emotions, and do not expect too much of themselves. They only expect the other person to be human.

Certainly all second marriages are not better than the first one. Many second marriages are replications of first marriages. All observers have noticed that often when a person marries a second time, he/she marries someone "just like" the first spouse. For example, a miserable wife of an alcoholic will marry an alcoholic the second time. A man who couldn't contain his wife's spending, will marry a spendthrift a second time. These people did not learn from their experience. They are in an "Almost Always" box and they need that other person to complete their psychological balance. They will be as unhappy in the second marriage as they were the first, but they will be no more enlightened about the basis of their unhappiness than they were when the first marriage was terminated.

Partnership development is essentially personal development.

Partnership development is essentially personal development. Once we have defined ourselves, we can define the kind of person with whom we wish to devote our time and attention.

Partnership maintenance is somewhat different. Keeping a marriage together is not enough. A world of difference exists between being happily married and *not* divorced. A happy marriage is a marriage which two people find rewarding. A couple works at a good marriage. They devote a lot of energy, thought, and resources to the relationship.

Rules cannot be generated which will ensure a good marriage, but some guidelines exist for establishing and maintaining a relationship which have stood the test of time. First and foremost is the need to be together, privately. A mature couple needs time to share private thoughts and experience each other. I do not mean talking about one's hobbies, or favorite foods, or special night spots, or other superficial things. I am talking about sharing one's self. What are your secret fears? What does your spouse value above all else? What are the things that make you feel good inside? What is your partner's belief about his/her worth? What does he/she think old age holds for the two of you?

A dinner out, or time with the children, or a holiday together is not the quality of togetherness that fosters the love relationship. These are important activities and they add enjoyment to being together, but building a quality relationship means giving individual attention without interruptions or distractions. A quality relationship means prolonged dialogue and focused attention; talking with each other, not to each other; and commitment of energy to understand each other.

The following activities are for a couple to use together as a way of examining the quality of their relationship.

Activity 7.6. Each of the partners completes for self the following sentences independently.

1. I am most confident about my ability to_____

_____

2. As I get older, I expect to _____

_____

3. My greatest disappointment was_____

_____

4. I feel really good when_____

_____

5. The thing I like most about myself is _____

_____

6. The thing I like most about my partner is _____

_____

7. Children are _____

_____

8. If I were to disagree with my partner, the disagreement would be over

_____

_____

9. I believe the thing my partner likes most about me is_____

_____

10. My partner is most confident about _____

_____

Activity 7.7. Now each is to complete independently the following sentences by writing in what he or she believes the partner would write.

1. I am most confident about my ability to_____

_____

2. As I get older, I expect to _____

_____

3. My greatest disappointment was_____

_____

4. I feel really good when_____

_____

5. The thing I like most about myself is _____

_____

6. The thing I like most about my partner is _____

_____

7. Children are _____

_____

8. If I were to disagree with my partner, the disagreement would be over

_____

_____

9. I believe the thing my partner likes most about me is_____

_____

10. My partner is most confident about _____

_____

Activity 7.8. Together compare your independent goals, concerns and dreams. Compare your preceptions of each other as recorded in Activity 7.7 with your partner's perceptions of self.

Activity 7.9. Another key to relationship maintenance is an awareness and an acceptance that one does not always have to be at one's best and does not expect the best always from one's partner. Human beings are cyclic in their performance. We need to understand the peaks and valleys, and how these two mesh.

One fairly simple way to get a fix on your emotional cycle is to make a systematic observation of your thoughts and feelings for several weeks. If a couple will do this and compare their record, they will be able to see their emotional ups and downs, and how to anticipate each other's moods.

Use a desk calendar (or a facsimile) to keep the log. Divide the day into two parts (one for recording thoughts and the other for recording feelings) and three time periods (early morning, noon, and early evening). An example calendar for two days observation might look like the illustrations in Figure 7.3.

MONDAY	*Thought*	*Feeling*
8 a.m.	Lots to do	Concerned
Noon:	Behind schedule	Hurried
6 p.m.	Much unfinished work	Unhappy anxious

TUESDAY		
8 a.m.:	Lovely day	Satisfied
Noon:	Unhappy news	Disappointed
6 p.m.	Relaxing and fun	Happy

Figure 7.3. Illustrations of Observations for Two Days.

Keep this record for four to six weeks. A comparison of the peaks and valleys will help a couple see how their moods fluctuate and how their cycles are different.

I would suggest a repeat of this activity every year or so. I think checkups on emotional health are important.

Activity 7.10. The quality of a relationship depends to a great extent on the ability of individuals as a couple to be congruent. Congruence has at least three parts: (1) Saying what you mean and meaning what you say; (2) accepting what one says as legitimate and responding to that, and (3) sending the same message verbally and nonverbally. A few exercises will help you check yourself on this score.

Sit in chairs back to back and discuss an important issue. Before responding, restate what the person said. An example of such a dialogue is as follows:

> WIFE: My mother is ill and I would like to go see her.
> HUSBAND: *Your mother is ill and you want to go see her,* but we do not have enough money for plane tickets this month for us to make the trip.
> WIFE: *We don't have enough money for plane fare this month for both of us to go,* but I could go and charge it on our credit card.
> HUSBAND: *You could go by yourself and you could charge it,* but his would mean that I could not go and even if you go by yourself, this will put a strain on the budget...

You will note that in such a dialogue one is forced to listen and communicate that the words were heard. Much attention and energy are needed to discuss in such a manner. But you will note that the words are assumed to be congruent—they are taken at face value. The speaker is allowed to complete the thought and the response is appropriate to the subject. I recommend that a couple spend as much time on this activity as it takes to become comfortable with talking in this fashion.

I recommend that a couple spend as much time on this activity as it takes to become comfortable with talking in this fashion.

Activity 7.11. This is an individual activity. A mirror will be used to help you evaluate the degree to which your verbal and nonverbal messages are congruent.

Stand before the mirror and without saying anything communicate the following:

1. love and pleasure

2. annoyance

3. worry

4. disapproval

5. uncertainty

6. sadness

Think of other emotions and try them. When you find yourself sending incongruent verbal and nonverbal responses, go back to the mirror and practice more. I think that, because of our cultural influences, women probably have more problems here than men.

Many everyday things will enhance a relationship and keep two people in tune. One major activity is the planning and use of the family resources. I believe a couple should perform as many purchasing tasks together as possible. This includes everything from major purchases, such as house and car, to minor purchases, such as weekly groceries. If two people keep current concerning expenditures and choices available little room will exist for disagreement on how money is spent. This is simple, yet money matters constitute a major source of friction for many couples.

If a couple has children either parent should speak for both parents and they should support each other's decisions. Disagreements concerning child rearing practices should be discussed in private. Quite likely the disagreement will be philosophical in nature with no right and wrong answers. The couple will want to avoid any appearance that one parent is less reasonable or more punishing than the other. Effective parents support each other, and they assist each other in their parenting role. If parents need help in this area, many excellent programs are available in almost every community. Most high schools and community schools have parent study groups, short courses and study materials.

All of the tasks which have to be performed just to keep the home running should be divided in some reasonable fashion. Effort should be made to discontinue sex role stereotyping in terms of routine tasks. Division of labor should be based on interest, skill and time. Nevertheless, regardless of task responsibility, both partners should be able to assume responsibility for the other's task without undue discomfort or problem. For example, if one generally pays the bills, the other person should stay current enough about the procedure to perform that task. This means that both partners know what is going on and both appreciate the contributions of the other. Routine tasks are no longer routine when they become a cooperative venture!

A couple should plan for as many common experiences as possible. Trying to keep together educationally, socially and spiritually, is important. Major experiences change lives. To explain the meaning of a peak experience is difficult if not possible. Thus, peak experiences should occur together if possible. For example, I would not recommend that one spouse attend a marathon growth group without the other.

For a couple to have common experiences is not always possible, but if the marriage is to remain satisfying, they will have to work out similar experiences.

For a couple to have **common** experiences is not always possible, but if the marriage is to remain satisfying, they will have to work out similar experiences. One example which we have all seen repeated is a divorce following on the heels of one partner's obtaining an advanced degree. This is especially true where one has worked to help the spouse finance college work. I do not believe that the degree, or the fact that one feels he/she is superior to the other, creates the situation that results in the divorce. I believe that the one working for and pursuing the degree undergoes major experiential changes which cannot be put into words and shared. Thus, a chasm exists. The breach cannot be closed by good intentions. People cannot **un**change. Therefore, a couple needs to plan change together. If for example, both partners cannot pursue a degree together, they might rotate their work study responsibilities. That is, one might work for one semester or one year while the other goes to school. Then they could exchange roles. Or, if one did not want a degree, that person could plan comparable learning experiences which would keep him/her involved in a similar experience and personal growth. Long hours at study make sense only to one who has experienced the joys and agonies of mastering new materials and gaining new insights.

168

If a couple would get rid of as many **shoulds** in their lives as possible it would be helpful. Doing something because one **should** is not very satisfying in the short run and in the long run produces anxieties and self doubt. Insisting that a husband or wife (or children even) do something because he or she **should** is even less satisfying and creates tensions in the family. To be congruent and know how one feels about a situation is difficult and even more difficult to behave on the basis of the expectations of someone else. To do so one has to guess what that person wants and analyze that person's evaluation of the behavior. One is forever on the defensive under such pressure. One is forever trying to win approval and acceptance from the significant other person. Disapproval is interpreted as lack of worth and, thus, a lowering of self-esteem occurs. Working under **shoulds** and **oughts** is counterproductive to development, growth and satisfaction.

The Brents, Leon and Evelyn, epitomize the effects a strong feeling of "should" can have on the growth of the individuals and the manner in which it limits the marriage and family relationships. Leon and Evelyn were married when they were quite young. They *Leon* were from upper mobile blue-collar working families who *Evelyn* wanted more for their children than they had for them- *Brent* selves. They wanted their children to go to college and not have to work so hard. They urged them to study and "amount to something."

Both Leon and Evelyn attended a small church-affiliated college where they were able to work to defray part of their college expenses. Though they were working and taking full academic loads, both were student leaders and involved in a variety of religious and social activities. With motivations which were based on their strong feelings of **should,** they competed quite successfully with their peers, both inside and outside the academic areas of college. No particular surprise was the fact that upon graduation, Evelyn was able to land a position as a sixth grade teacher. Leon landed a job he highly prized in the office of the State Senator. They were sure they could get ahead if they would "keep their wagons hitched to the stars." Their values were similar in that both believed that they "should work hard" and that anything worth doing was "worth doing well!"

That was sixteen years ago. They are still dedicated to their goals, that is, trying to reach their stars. Leon is now the district constituency advocate for one of the most powerful congressmen in the state. Evelyn is still a sixth grade teacher, but more importantly she is Leon's wife, or more accurately, the wife of Congressman x's Constituency Advocacy Representative.

Leon works long hours and is as close to the constituencies as the telephone. This situation means that as a family they have few uninterrupted evenings. This situation also means that as a couple they have almost no time for themselves. Even weekends, except during church hours when they are attending worship services together, they are tied up with calls, visits, and/or serving a constituent (for the Congressman). Their life was very difficult and demanding, but Leon feels their life is a very important "mission." He is serving people, and he believes this is why human beings were put in the world.

Representing the Congressman as he does, Leon feels he and his wife should participate broadly in the community services and offer leadership to civic activities. The children too, ages twelve and fourteen, are told that they have a responsibility to set a good example and reflect well on the Congressman. They dress and behave (in public) as their parents believe they should dress and behave. So do Leon and Evelyn. As they say, they are "always on display."

Leon and Evelyn have never taken a (non-work) vacation together. They have been on trips together, but these were trips which they needed to take to represent the Congressman.

Leon believes he will never be worthy of the faith his employer places in him. His greatest fear is that he or his family will embarrass the Congressman. Evelyn understands this. She tries to be the person she should be—the kind of person Leon feels she should be. With their modest income they have difficulty in presenting an appropriate front to the public. But she tries. She keeps an immaculate house. Their clothes, while few, are appropriate and clean. She likes to paint, but has never had time to do so. Painting is too messy and she has to keep herself and her house presentable. She goes to school in the summer and picks up enough college credit to keep her teacher's certificate renewed, but she doesn't feel she can afford to work toward a master's degree. Leon doesn't especially want her to anyway. He sees her job as secondary to his. According to Leon, she is his wife first, and she teaches to supplement the income. While Evelyn likes to think she is a good teacher, she does agree that being a wife and mother comes first. They present a solid front. They represent the Congressman well.

Evelyn is anxious (high strung) and underweight. With responsibility for the boys, her school, and a week's conference each summer in "staff" training with her husband's colleagues and their wives, she has little time for herself. She sees no way to change this because these activities are things she has to do—or at least should do. The only relief which she sees ahead is when the boys get through college—then she may be able to quit work.

The oldest son is in the eighth grade. Like his dad, he is a perfectionist. He is never quite ready to tackle a task, and is never quite satisfied with his performance. He spends a great deal of time justifying his behavior, lobbying for his point-of-view, and asking questions. The youngest, a sixth grader, is an overambitious child who has given up. He makes poor grades, and does not get along with his peers. His parents are worried about him. They don't understand what his problem is.

The Brents live for others and through others. They judge what they should do by what they think someone else expects. They are externally controlled, and in their position, more responsive to the pressures of others than most people would be.

Leon cannot separate himself from his work. He cannot separate his family from himself or his work. All of these things and people are confused, so he attempts to make sense out of his life by controlling himself and his family with *shoulds.* These "shoulds" are deductions he has made from what he has been told and what he believes about others. No matter how much he succeeds he will always feel inadequate. Rather than enjoy his family, he lives in mortal fear that they will make an error. They can never enjoy who they are because they are trying so hard to become what they perceive they should be. For the members in the Brent family, the idealized self and real self are independent. In Figure 7.4, I have depicted this type of individual, and in Figure 7.5. a more fully-functioning individual who is less externally controlled is depicted. The idealized self and the real self are fairly consistent for the person with high self esteem.

I am arguing for making peace with yourself and your world as a first step in developing comfort and enjoyment in this world. Comfortable individuals who are basically satisfied with themselves make comfortable and enjoyable mates. Their *shoulds* are recognized as cultural expectations transmitted through parents, schools, and church. These are acceptable as representing the idealized culture (see Chapter 1

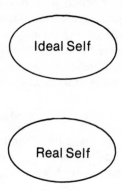

Figure 7.4. Externally Controlled Person With Low Self-Esteem.

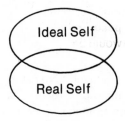

Figure 7.5. Self-Directed Person With High Self-Esteem.

for a discussion of the difference between the real and ideal culture). The healthy individual negotiates a working relationship between these idealized values and ones that serve his/her needs in the real world. The healthy individual is self-accepting. The fully-functioning individual appreciates humanness and is most comfortable with behavior that is congruent with his/her feelings.

We have moved away from a simple agrarian society where roles were defined and meeting survival needs required most of the attention of the family. We have moved into a basically urban society with the resulting dislodgement of traditional sex roles. The family is much less dependent on each other than they are on the other social systems, especially the economic system, which provide us work and services.

172

This change gives us time and freedom to work on human relationships within the family, while at the same time threatens us with an information overload which may destroy our very ability to relate to other human beings. Like a computer, the individual's system can process or assimilate just so many inputs or stimuli. Thus, modern society mandates that we establish priorities for our attention and responses. I am proposing that the family be given the basic priority for our psychic energy. Let us respond to these significant people with the necessary time and sustained attention to hear, understand, and help. Since most contacts (in this urban, intense world) must be limited, ignored and kept superficial, the family has become more important to the individual. The individual must look to the family for that intimate acceptance each of us needs to be human.

I am also arguing for parents to model the congruent self acceptance needed for ego development to sustain us in a rather impersonal world. We do not need to pay the same kind of intense attention to every concern that we do to the relationship concerns. I believe every person in a family should have some few minutes of *undivided attention* from both parents every day. This time does not have to be long in duration but it does have to be intense and uninterrupted. One way to conserve energy for these important human relations tasks is to set a schedule for daily activities which the family does without undue interaction and concern. Such things as cooking, cleaning, and laundering come under this category. This routine does not require attention of significant others which can be better used for meaningful dialogue and family activities.

Finally, we can live more creatively if we have expectations for ourselves and treat ourselves as we want to treat others. For example, Joan expects some uninterrupted time each day. Her children and husband respect this privacy. If she is in her study, for example, they do not interrupt her (unless a real emergency arises). When Joan comes from the study she is ready to be involved with the family. For a parent to communicate these expectation or rules is not difficult.

Joan

Living creatively means being involved. A certain spontaneity is necessary to remain flexible enough to be involved in the world. Involvement in the process of being is the best possible attitude for trusting that world which is predictable but not guaranteed. If one is involved with the family. For a parent to communicate these expectations or rules is not difficult.

FRAMEWORK FOR ANALYSIS

The philosophical framework for consideration in a second marriage and possibly merger of two families is summarized in the questions and statements that follow. The statements are in list form, first to provide philosophy and beliefs explicitly, and, second, to enable family members to study and discuss issues that may affect their relationships.

Since some readers can be expected to be concerned primarily with marriage relationships and other readers primarily with family relationships, the remarks are organized under two headings. Topic A offers ideas applicable to second marriages and Topic B is primarily relevant to merged families. The questions and statements may be used as a framework for analysis prior to or within a second marriage.

Topic A—ITEMS TO CONSIDER

1. *To what extent have we individually resolved our personal problems?*

    Culturally speaking, a second marriage is built upon the failure of a first marriage. Such a concept is itself a negative force which impacts the second marriage. Young "first" married receive psychological support and personal well wishes from family and friends; whereas, older "second" married tend to begin their lives together in the midst of disrupted families, confused relatives, and dissolved friendships. Thus, second marriages are likely to magnify personal problems and, if left unresolved, will affect adversely the couple's relationship.

2. *What are the indicators that each of us are interpersonally mature?*

    The quality of a marriage relationship is a representation of the intrapersonal functioning of two individuals. A marriage can be no more effective than the personal effectiveness of the two people involved. Therefore, the basic ingredient for a successful second marriage is a marriage between two personally successful individuals.

3. *How will this second marriage enable me (us) to be able to think and act differently instead of my (our) old behavior patterns?*

New relationships make underlying problems obvious. Personality problems seem to surface with a second marriage and the development of a new family system. Conversely, a second marriage offers a second chance to apply mature thinking and experience to the structure and design of a social system which is satisfying and fulfilling.

4. *What evidence do we have that each of us will be able to own and share our feelings?*

A successful or mentally healthy person is an accepting person who is open to new experiences. Indeed, the person with high self-regard owns and accepts his or her feelings as valid, appreciates expressions of uniqueness, and accommodates individual differences.

5. *Can I (we) openly communicate when failure is facing me (us)?*

The most dangerous problem in any marriage is the failure to communicate. Second marriage partners seem to be particularly susceptible to silence in the face of difficulties. Clear communication and adequate information are necessary if a positive relationship is to be developed and maintained.

6. *Have we discussed and agreed upon appropriate behavior which we will expect in the second marriage?*

Individual perceptions of appropriate behavior in a second marriage are to some extent extrapolated from previous marriage experiences and role situations. These perceptions produce attitudes and motivations, known as personal agenda, which may be dysfunctional to the new marriage relationship. Unfinished business and conflict are thus transferred on this personal level to an unrelated situation and effect the quality of relationship which can be developed.

7. *By what manner will we enable the personality changes in each other during the second marriage to be accepted rather than to produce crisis?*

Each person chooses his or her own feelings, and every person has the capacity for change. Insecure people resist personal change because they are afraid of the unknown. Because insecure people are afraid of the unknown, they do not want their spouses to change and feel threatened when change occurs. No one can actually control another person and no one can force another to change. Nevertheless, if one partner chooses to change and does so, every family will be affected and will themselves change their behavior. Thus, family disruptions or family crises occur when either partner makes a major personality shift.

8. *What is our plan for seeking professional help if either of us sense a communication decrease between us?*

Divorce is testimony that change has occurred. Divorce is a process and, thus it occurs over time. While the legal act of divorce is identifiable, the initial stage in the process is less specific. Usually, a couple experiences dissatisfaction in terms of quality and amount of communication during the early phase of the process. Communication suffers because energy is being drained from the marriage relationship and redirected into some other relationships, activities or concerns. During this early period, increased dialogue is needed to counter the trend and develop mutual support and establish common goals. Since individuals tend to close off conversation in the face of conflict, quite likely a couple will need professional help to facilitate communication.

9. *What are our commitments to making this second marriage an on-going evolving partnership?*

Life expectancy has increased drastically. "Until death. . ."has taken on new meaning and many individuals and couples simply are not willing to "tough it out." Time is seen as too limited not to enjoy it to the fullest, and too long to tolerate an unhappy marriage.

10. *To what extent do we see each other as equal?*

When a second marriage is between compeers the outcome is likely to be synergestic. Compeers are equal. A compeer relationship is possible between two individuals who are self-sufficient with positive self-images.

11. *What are our plans for making the marriage an opportunity for each other to develop?*

Marriage relationships tend to be representations of relationships modeled as children. A few lucky people learned to be effective partners, or compeers, some became manipulators, or playmates, and some controllers, or checkmates. Since behavior is learned, a person can change. A second marriage offers a new opportunity to develop the type of relationship an individual or couple desires.

12. Which is more important to each of us in this second marriage—the process or the end result?

An individual has a limited amount of energy to expend on all relationships. A marriage relationship requires a large investment of energy. The relationship is always dynamic and changing; thus, obtaining a specific goal is less important than the process used for obtaining goals. The quality of the process is the quality of the marriage.

Topic B—MERGED FAMILIES: RELATIONSHIPS AMONG MEMBERS

1. What evidence is present to indicate that each family member will feel secure in the merged family?

The dynamics in a merged family are not appreciably different from the dynamics of a family comprised of both natural parents. All behavior is purposeful and appropriate from the perceptual reference of the family member. Secure people who feel accepted and accepting of others produce a functional family; whereas, insecure people who attempt to control their environment by controlling others, produce dysfunctional family systems.

2. What are illustrations of how the merged family will gain strength from the usual cultural conditions imposed?

Merged families may experience cultural conditions which make the parenting role difficult for one or both of the spouses. For example, a teacher may turn to the natural parent for advice, or relatives may see, and refer to, a new spouse as a person added to an intact family system. Such cultural attitudes have an influence on a family, but these attitudes do not make nor do they destroy the family. Parents, expecting these cultural experiences, can depersonalize events and garner strength from their mutual goal to develop a new family system which offers satisfaction to all of its participants.

3. *Under what conditions have the merged family members demonstrated open family discussions?*

Cultural mores tend to influence family interaction when children of a previous marriage are involved. For example, the use of the word "step" in reference to parent connotes a relationship different from natural parent. Legend and stories of "step" parents create an image of cruelty and fear and make one wary. These cultural expressions need to be countered, at the family level, with a positive program or plan which will neutralize their impact. Family discussions (family hour or family council) is one of the most effective procedures. Discussions or conversations are crucial to good relationships. Personal interactions involving all family members are necessary if a new family social system is to merge from the two or more previous family systems making up the new family.

4. *When have we as parents cooperatively reinforced predictable consequences in the children?*

A family is a social system. Parents are the social engineers. If the parents reinforce *eccentric* behavior the child will experience success in the family and failure in other social systems. Successful parents will reinforce *predictable* consequences so that a child will gain skill in estimating and anticipating the outcomes of his or her behavior.

5. *What are our attitudes toward seeking professional help in working with the children?*

When the family social system is not functioning adequately to meet the needs of every family member, parents will find it beneficial to seek professional help. An outsider, who is trained in relationship skills, can assist the family in seeking new goals and establishing ways of relating and can offer support during the disrupting transitional period when change is taking place. A fully functioning family is quite flexible, and creativity is fostered in such an atmosphere.

178

6. What are the role expectations of the various merged family members?

Sex role stereotyping and cultural expectations are limiting factors in personality and relationship development. A new marriage is an ideal time to reconsider what tasks are appropriately performed by various family members and how role expectations can be expanded and enriched.

INDEX

ABOUT THE AUTHOR

Dr. Jonell H. Kirby (Ed.D.) is professor of counseling and psychology in the counseling and guidance program at West Virginia College of Graduate Studies in Institute, West Virginia. Dr. Kirby has a long list of professional experiences and interests in family systems, group dynamics and problem solving.

She began her career teaching in public schools in Georgia, has been a visiting professor at Syracuse University, New York, and the University of Georgia, Athens. Dr. Kirby has been director of the Counseling Center at Augusta College, Georgia; director of instruction in Cleveland, Georgia; associate professor at West Virginia University; has worked in the Counseling and Guidance Program at West Virginia College of Graduate Studies in many capacities and is now Professor at the College.

Dr. Kirby is a member of the American Personnel and Guidance Association; American Psychological Association; Association for Specialists in Group Work; and, Association for Counselor Education and Supervision.

Dr. Kirby has participated in both national and international activities a member of the North Central Commission; as consultant to overseas workshops in Portugal, Australia, Brazil, Canada, Egypt, Mexico, England and France; as a member of West Virginia Advisory Council on Professional Development of Educational Personnel; and, as a member of the Standing Committee on Continuing Education (State Advisory Council).

Dr. Kirby has co-authored *Handbook of Guidance Services, Group Guidance: A Critical Incidents Approach,* and *Manual for Users of Standardized Tests.* She has contributed articles to professional journals, chapters in books, and has written papers and given presentations to national professional meetings. Dr. Kirby has participated in technical reports with both Project CARE and Project DRIVE.

Dr. Kirby is married to Joe E. Kirby, (Ed.D), associate professor of educational administration and director for administrative and field services at West Virginia College of Graduate Studies, Institute, West Virginia.

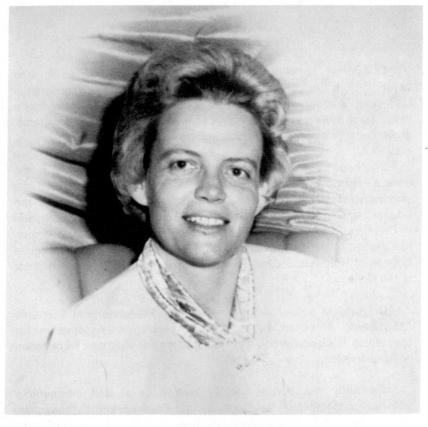

Jonell H. Kirby

DATE DUE

GAYLORD			PRINTED IN U.S.A.